The 2011 Pritzker Architecture Prize
EDUARDO SOUTO DE MOURA

The 2011 Pritzker Architecture Prize
EDUARDO SOUTO DE MOURA

Edited by Joana de Mira Corrêa (Senior Architect)

DESIGN MEDIA PUBLISHING LIMITED

CONTENTS

About Eduardo Souto de Moura

Eduardo Souto de Moura was born in Porto, Portugal in 1952. His father was a doctor (ophthalmologist) and his mother was a home maker.

Following his early years at the Italian School, Souto de Moura enrolled in the School of Fine Arts in Porto, where he began as an art student, studying sculpture, but eventually achieving his degree in architecture. He credits a meeting with Donald Judd in Zurich for the switch from art to architecture. While still a student, he worked for architect Noé Dinis and then Álvaro Siza, the latter for five years. While studying and working with his professor of urbanism, Architect Fernandes de Sá, he received his first commission, a market project in Braga which has since been demolished because of changing business patterns.

After 2 years of military service he won the competition for the Cultural Centre in Porto, the beginning of his career as an independent architect.

He is frequently invited as a guest professor to Lausanne and Zurich in Switzerland as well as Harvard in the United States. These guest lectures at universities and seminars over the years have afforded him the opportunity to meet many colleagues in the field, among them Jacques Herzog and Aldo Rossi.

Along with his architecture practice, Souto de Moura is a professor at the University of Oporto, and is a visiting professor at Geneva, Paris-Belleville, Harvard, Dublin and the ETH Zurich and Lausanne.

Often described as a neo-Miesian, but one who constantly strives for originality, Souto de Moura has achieved much praise for his exquisite use of materials - granite, wood, marble, brick, steel, concrete - as well as his unexpected use of colour. Souto de Moura is clear on his view of the use of materials, saying, "I avoid using endangered or protected species. I think we should use wood in moderation and replant our forests as we use the wood. We have to use wood because it is one of the finest materials available."

In an interview with Croquis, he explained, "I find Mies increasingly fascinating... There is a way of reading him which is just to regard him as a minimalist. But he always oscillated between classicism and neoplasticism... You only have to remember the last construction of his life, the IBM building, with that powerful travertine base that he drilled through to produce a gigantic door. Then on the other hand, he arrived in Barcelona and did two pavilions, didn't he? One was abstract and neo plastic and the other one was classical, symmetrical with closed corners...He was experimenting. He was already so modern that he was 'post'."

Souto de Moura acknowledges the Miesian influence, speaking of his Burgo Tower, but refers people to something written by Italian journalist and critic, Francesco Dal Co, "it's better not to be original but good, rather than wanting to be very original and bad."

At a series of forums called the Holcim Forum on sustainable architecture, Souto de Moura stated, "For me, architecture is a global issue. There is no ecological architecture, no intelligent architecture, no sustainable architecture - there is only good architecture. There are always problems we must not neglect; for example, energy, resources, costs, social aspects - one must always pay attention to all these."

01 S.E.C. Cultural Centre - "Casa das Artes"

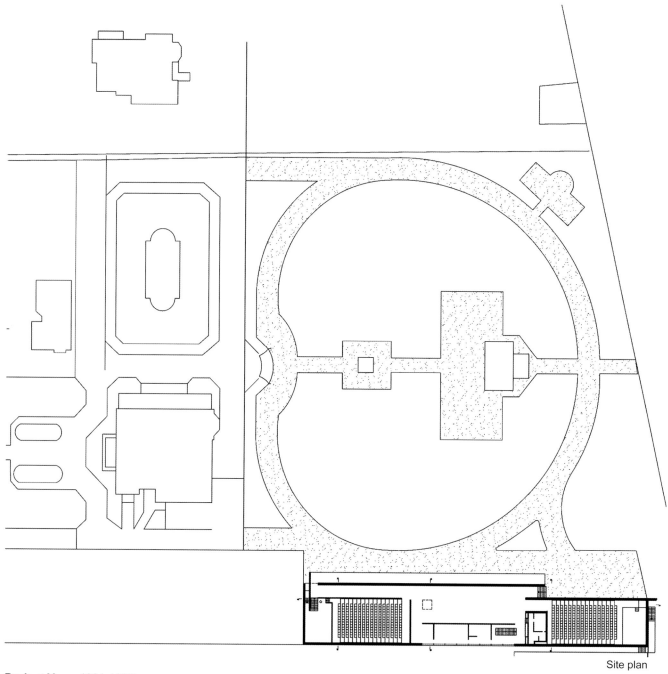

Site plan

Project Year: 1981-1985
Construction Year: 1988-1991
Address: Rua António Cardoso, 175
Location: Porto, Portugal
Client: Secretaria de Estado da Cultura
Collaborators: João Carreira, Luísa Penha
Structural Consultants: João Maria A. Sobreira
Electrical Consultants: José Sousa Guedes
Mechanical Consultants: Constantino Matos Campos
General Contractor: Soares da Costa
Photographer: Luís Ferreira Alves

"The castle was big, though, wasn't it? And the angel was big, very big, even when right next to you?" Rilke, *Duíno Elegies*

Work was not allowed to interfere with the garden. Omitting was more important than proposing, filing and shaving was more important than designing, and simplicity more important than composition. The building is structured primarily by a concrete wall, and by another stone wall, adjusted and somewhat out of phase at the point of the doorway. A flat copper-plated roof rests on these walls. Work would begin two metres from the line of trees that we did not want to affect. There would be three sculptures. Regardless of their quality, we were interested in their location, and attitude in the place that they would participate in shaping and making too. They are all essential pieces in the definition and codification of the three sectors: the Auditorium, the Exhibition Hall and the Cinema. The first sculpture will rest on the wall that comes from outside the garden and, upon entering into the auditorium, makes the interior stage or theatre. The second sculpture will be in the entrance to the exhibition hall, serving as the emblematic doorway to the Centre as well as capping off the elevation. The third will have the cinema as its backdrop, placed near the wall that separates the Cultural Centre from the nine-storey-high tower...

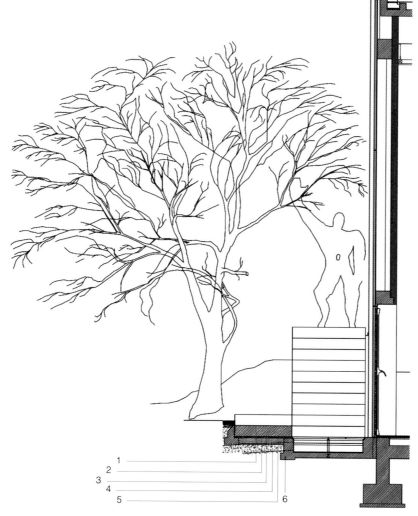

Section 1
1. Yellow granite
2. Bedding mortar
3. Concrete screed
4. Gravel
5. Connecting pipe to the collector ¢ 125mm
6. Concrete box

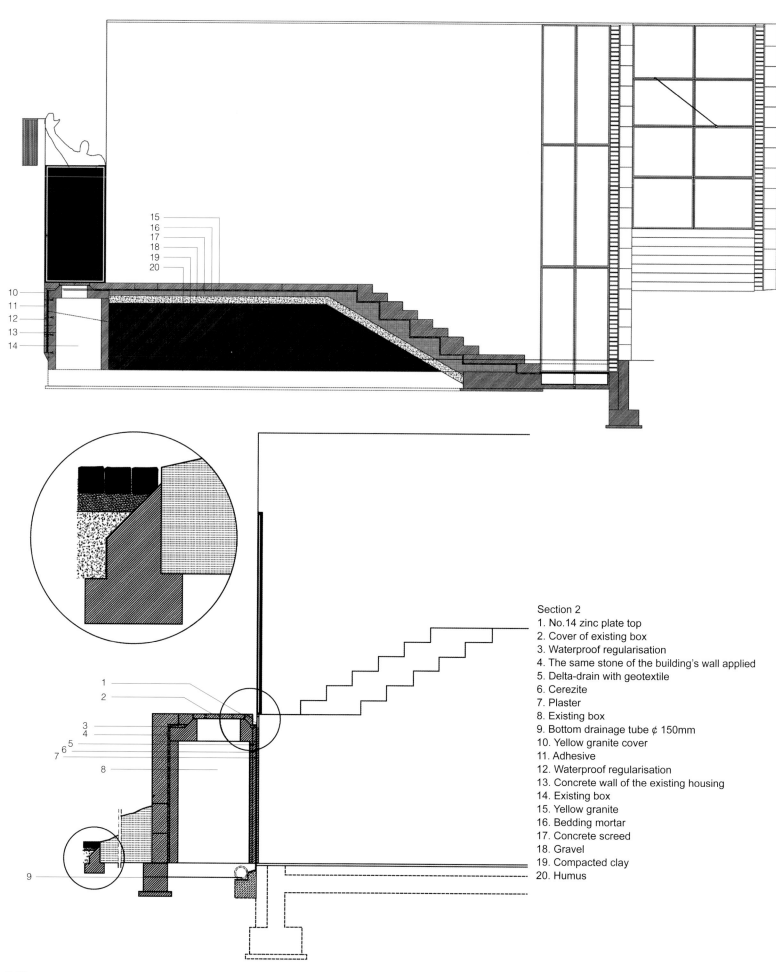

Section 2
1. No.14 zinc plate top
2. Cover of existing box
3. Waterproof regularisation
4. The same stone of the building's wall applied
5. Delta-drain with geotextile
6. Cerezite
7. Plaster
8. Existing box
9. Bottom drainage tube ¢ 150mm
10. Yellow granite cover
11. Adhesive
12. Waterproof regularisation
13. Concrete wall of the existing housing
14. Existing box
15. Yellow granite
16. Bedding mortar
17. Concrete screed
18. Gravel
19. Compacted clay
20. Humus

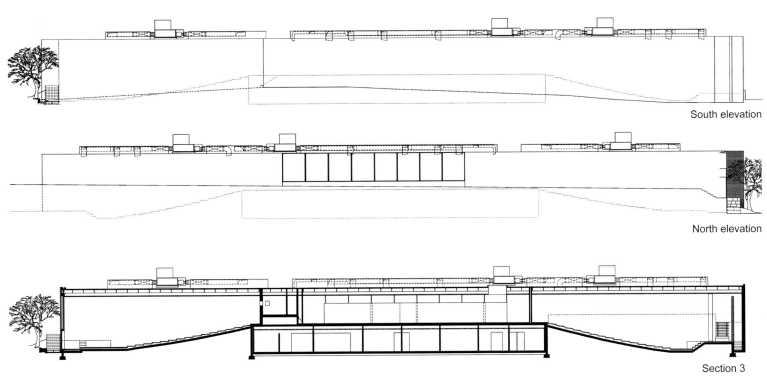

South elevation

North elevation

Section 3

013

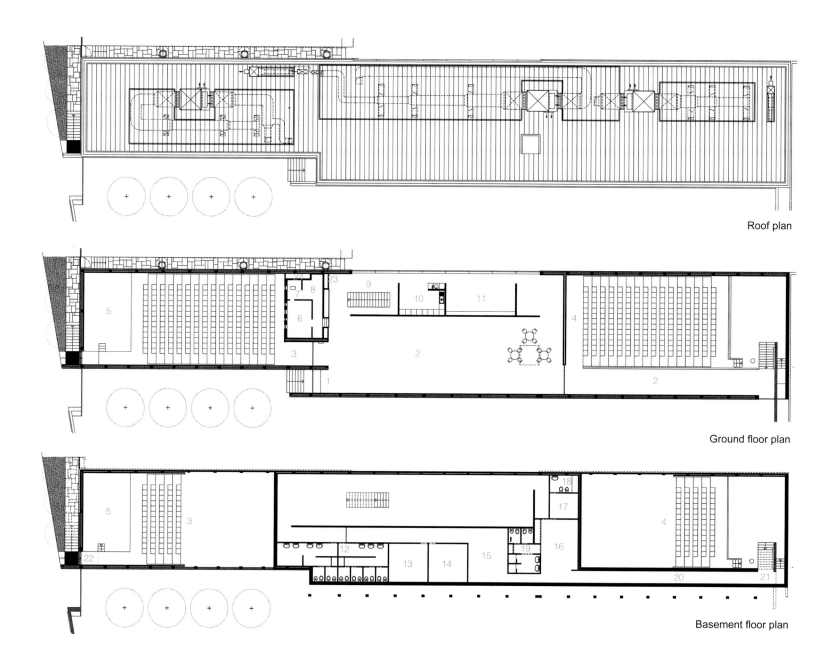

Roof plan

Ground floor plan

Basement floor plan

1. Entrance
2. Foyer/exhibitions
3. Cinematheque
4. Auditorium
5. Stage
6. Projection booth
7. Fire station
8. Winding booth
9. Secretary
10. Cabinet
11. Library
12. Public toilets
13. General collection
14. Book file
15. Film archive
16. Dressing room
17. Chamber
18. Bathroom
19. Bathroom for artists
20. Gallery at access
21. Command of light/sound
22. Emergency exit
23. Wardrobe technician
24. Conduct

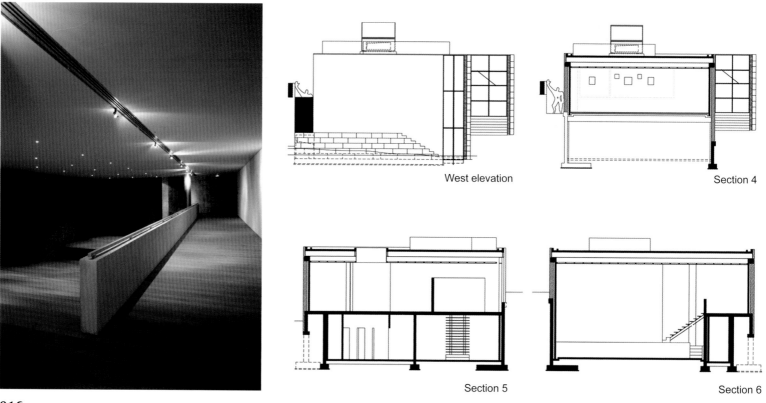

West elevation

Section 4

Section 5

Section 6

02 Conversion of the Santa Maria do Bouro Convent into a State Inn

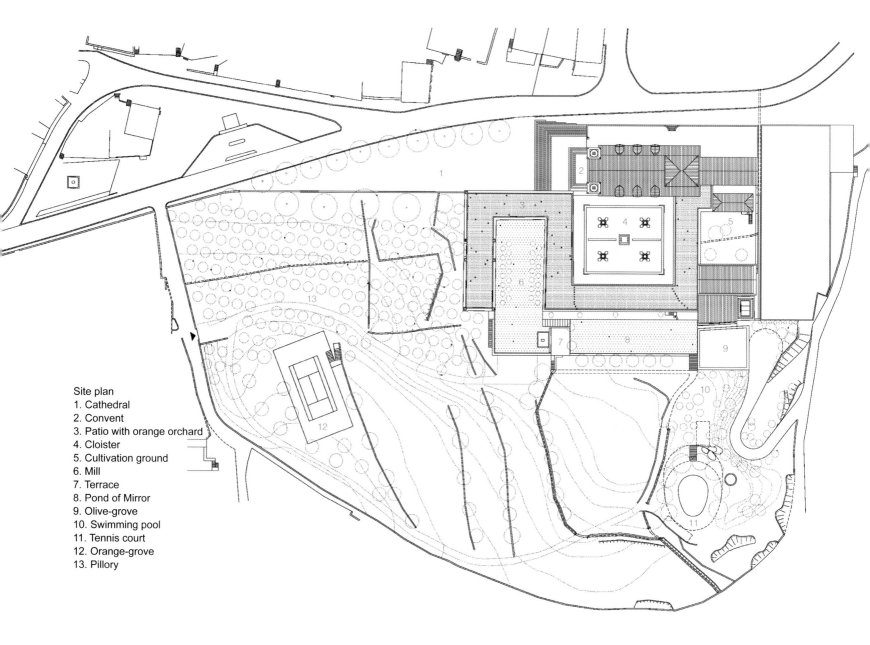

Site plan
1. Cathedral
2. Convent
3. Patio with orange orchard
4. Cloister
5. Cultivation ground
6. Mill
7. Terrace
8. Pond of Mirror
9. Olive-grove
10. Swimming pool
11. Tennis court
12. Orange-grove
13. Pillory

Co-author: Humberto Vieira
Project Year: 1989
Construction Year: 1997
Address: Bouro, Amares
Location: Braga, Portugal
Client: Enatur
Collaborators: Manuela Lara, Marie Clement,
Ana Fortuna, Pedro Valente
Structural Consultants: G.O.P.
Electrical Consultants: G.O.P.
Mechanical Consultants: Gestão Energia Térmica
General Contractor: Soares da Costa
Photographer: Luís Ferreira Alves
Building Size: 7,300 m²
Cost: 7,980,766.35 Euros

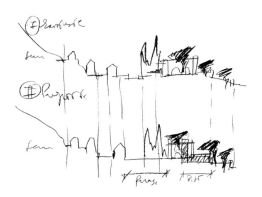

This project aims to adapt, or rather, to make use of the stones available to build a new building. It is a new building, in which various voices and functions (some already registered, other still to be constructed) intervene; it is not a reconstruction of the building in its original form. For this project, the ruins are more important than the "Convent"; they are open and manipulable, just as the building was during its history. This attitude is not meant to express or represent an exceptional case justifying some original manifesto, but rather to abide by a rule of architecture, more or less unchanging throughout time. During the design process, lucidity was sought for between the form and the programme. Faced with two possible paths, the architect chose to reject the pure and simple consolidation of the ruin for the sake of contemplation, opting instead for the introduction of new materials, uses, forms and functions "entre les choses", as Corbusier said. The "picturesque" is a question of fate, not part of a project or programme.

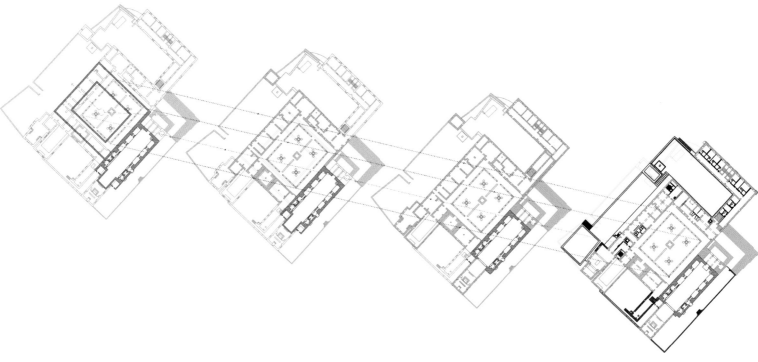

Axonometric drawing

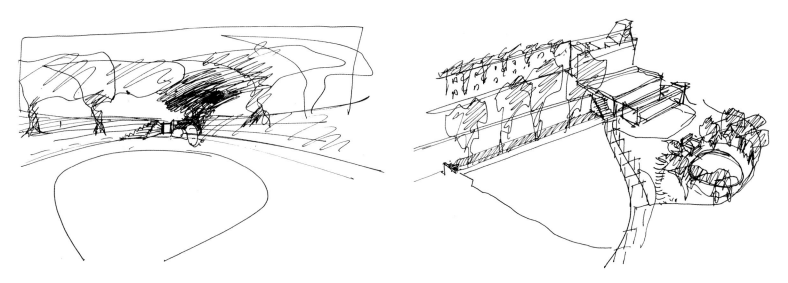

1) Claustro.
2) Aurora.
3) Pavimento.

022

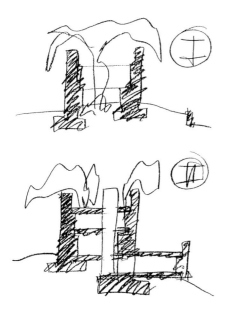

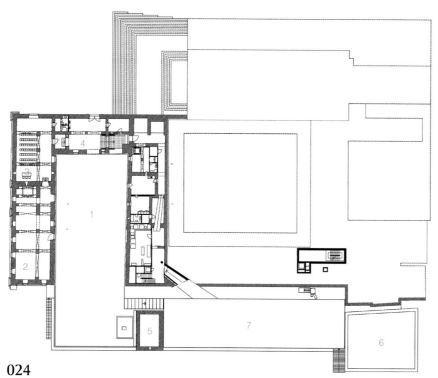

Ground floor plan (Left)
1. Patio with orange orchard
2. Show room
3. Auditorium
4. Entrance hall
5. Mill
6. Pond of Mirror
7. Terrace

Section 1 (Below)
1. Blackout gutter
2. Yellow brass window frame
3. Compressed band
4. Locker
5. Double glass 6+6+6mm
6. Hinge

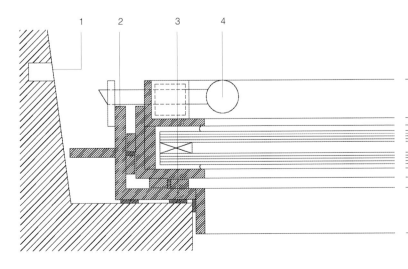

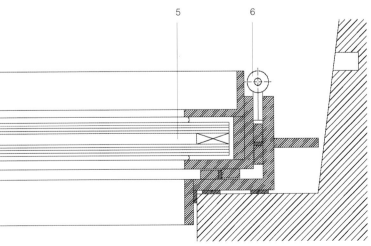

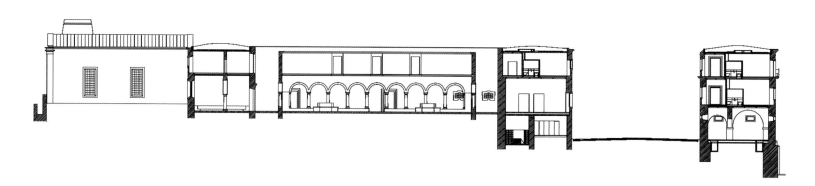

Section 2

Corredor dos Quartos.

First floor plan
1. Cathedral
2. Void above cloister
3. Void above patio
4. Guest rooms
5. Lounge
6. Patio with orange orchard
7. Terrace
8. Living room
9. Billiard room
10. Dining room
11. Restaurant
12. Chapter room
13. Sacristy
14. Cultivation ground
15. Pond of Mirror

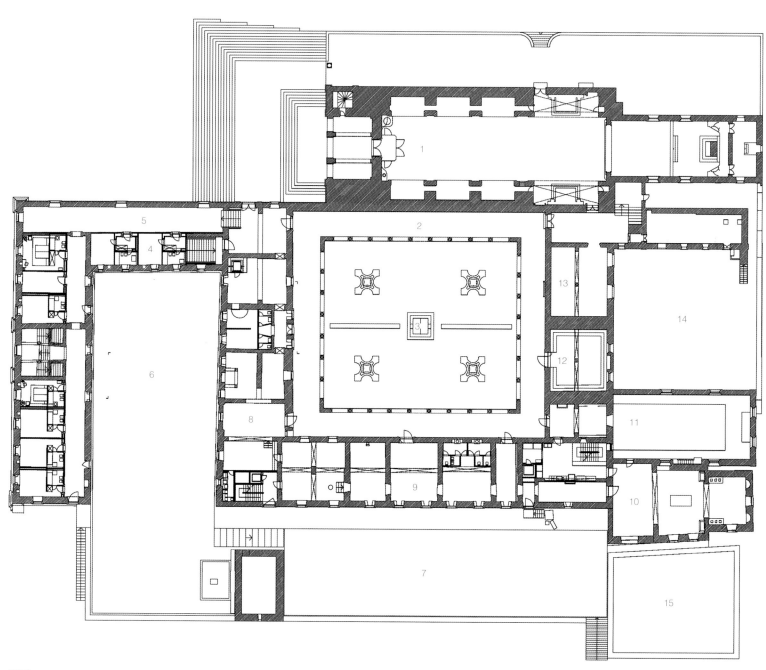

03 Burgo Tower

Project Year: Phase 1: 1991, Phase 2: 2003
Construction Year: Under construction
Address: Av. Boavista
Locality: Porto, Portugal
Client: Burgo Fundiários, S.A.
Collaborators:
Phase 1 (1991/1995): Teresa Gonçalves, Adriano Pimenta,
António Dias, Filipe Pinto da Cruz, Francisco Cunha,
Francisco Vieira de Campos, Graça Correia,
Manuela Lara, Marie Clement, Nuno Rodrigues Pereira,
Pedro Mendes, Pedro Reis, Silvia Alves
Phase 2 (2003/2004): Silvia Alves, Diogo Guimarães,
Manuel Vasconcelos, Diogo Morais, Susana Monteiro
Structural consultants: AFAssociados
Hidraulic consultants: Vitor Abrantes Consultores
Electrical consultants: Rodrigues Gomes & Associados
Mechanical consultants: AFAssociados
General contractor: San José
Photographer: Luís Ferreira Alves

The site is located where the Avenida da Boavista breaks into discontinuous sections; it is the biggest straight-line avenue in Portugal that extends from "Casa da Música" till the Sea in West. The solution consists in a level platform which incorporates two nearby volumes which recast in different scales. A low ribbon-like building allows for the enclosure more close to approximate the sought-after anonymity. The tower, set back from the avenue, rises up from the platform, waiting for further and future works of architecture still to come. This office complex opens a large square between the two buildings, one horizontal and the other vertical. The square is occupied by a big sculpture by the Porto architect/sculptor Nadir de Afonso. The buildings were drawn with very simple shapes, following the influences of Mies and the Chicago buildings. The main interest about the building is its façade. Its skin is composed out of a single module that wraps all the volumes. That module was studied so it could fit on two different ways creating a glass façade and an opaque façade. The building was described by the Pirtzker jury as "…two buildings side by side, one vertical and one horizontal with different scales, in dialogue with each other and the urban landscape." Souto de Moura commented that "a twenty storey office tower is an unusual project for me. I began my career building single family houses."

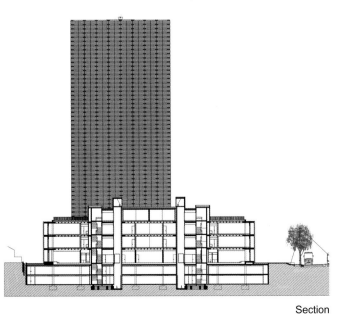

Section

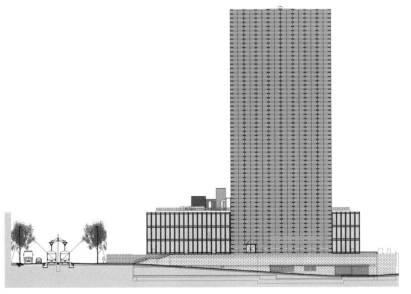

West elevation

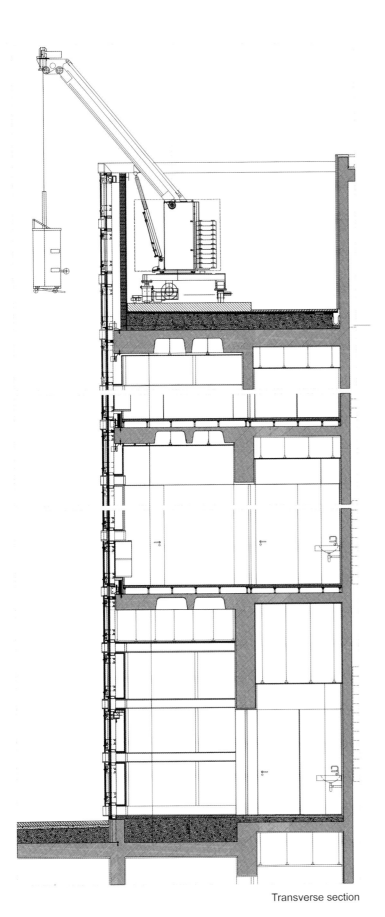

Transverse section

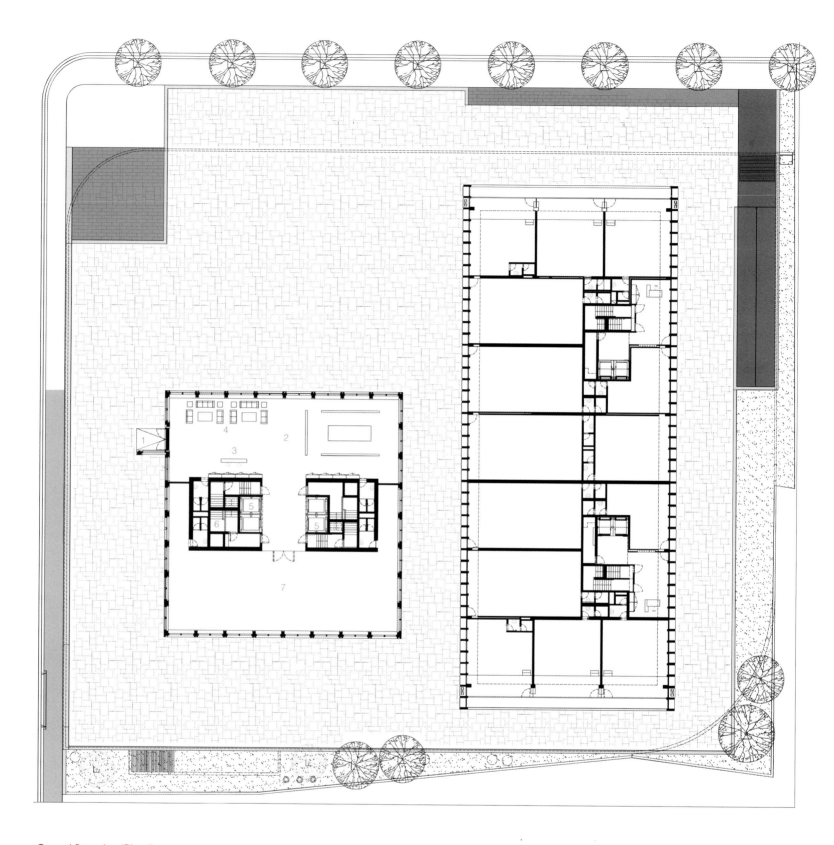

Ground floor plan (Plaza)
1. Entrance
2. Entrance hall
3. Reception
4. Waiting area
5. Elevator
6. Stairs
7. Trade

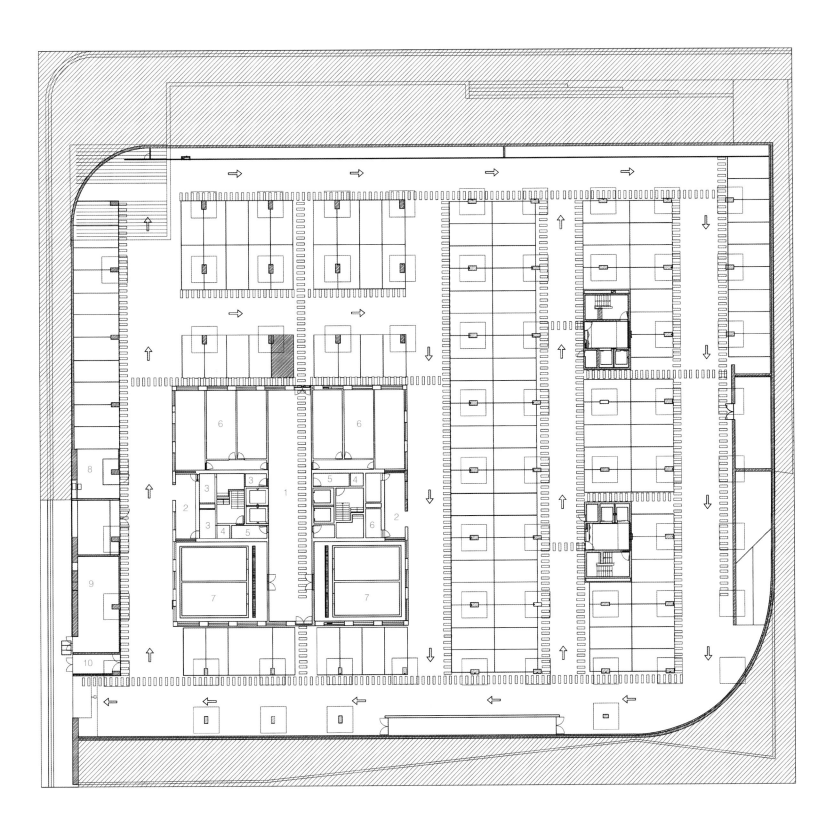

Typical floor plan
1. Atrium elevators
2. Atrium
3. Technical area
4. Bandstand
5. Antechamber
6. Tidy room
7. Drinking water supplies
8. HVAC technique installation
9. Generator
10. Garbage

041

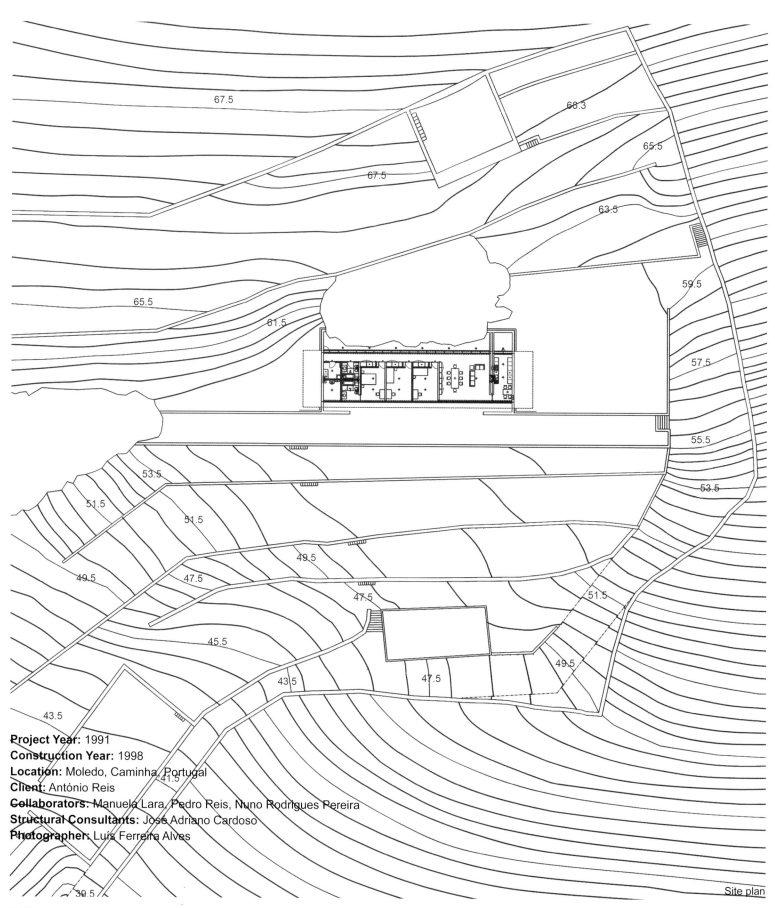

67.5

68.3

65.5

67.5

63.5

59.5

65.5

61.5

57.5

55.5

53.5

51.5

51.5

53.5

49.5

51.5

47.5

49.5

47.5

45.5

47.5

43.5

43.5

41.5

Project Year: 1991
Construction Year: 1998
Location: Moledo, Caminha, Portugal
Client: António Reis
Collaborators: Manuela Lara, Pedro Reis, Nuno Rodrigues Pereira
Structural Consultants: José Adriano Cardoso
Photographer: Luís Ferreira Alves

39.5

Site plan

After the experience at the Baião House, I felt that it would be more natural, in Portugal, to design wooden frames. To this end, the roof has to be exposed to view, declaring itself a new object, visible as if fallen from the sky. The project set out to redesign another, earlier house, analogous in terms of site, programme and materials. One exception, one aspect that was not a redesign, is that we had to reconstruct the hillside with new retaining walls and platforms, and this cost more than the house itself. "Le coeur a des raisons..." The client, as an intelligent man, was in agreement, and during seven years the house progressively gained in autonomy, passing from the redesign to the specific design for the occupants and the site which we progressively discovered and modified.

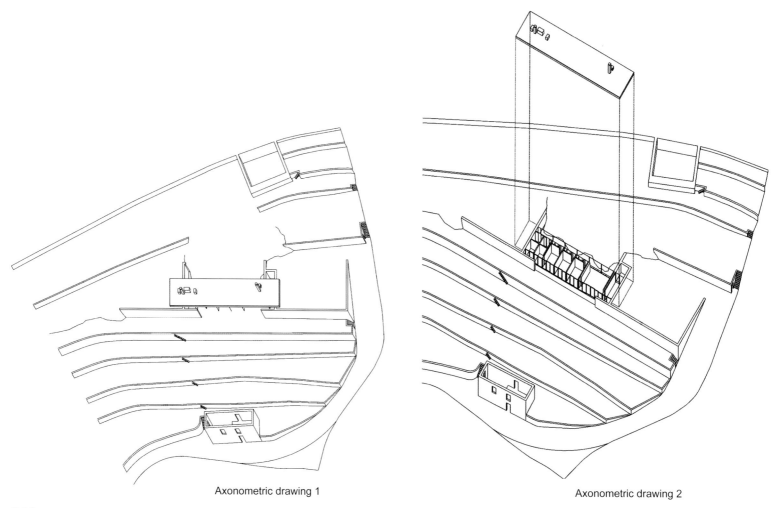

Axonometric drawing 1   Axonometric drawing 2

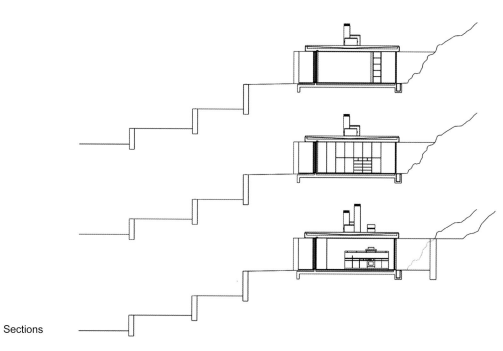

Sections

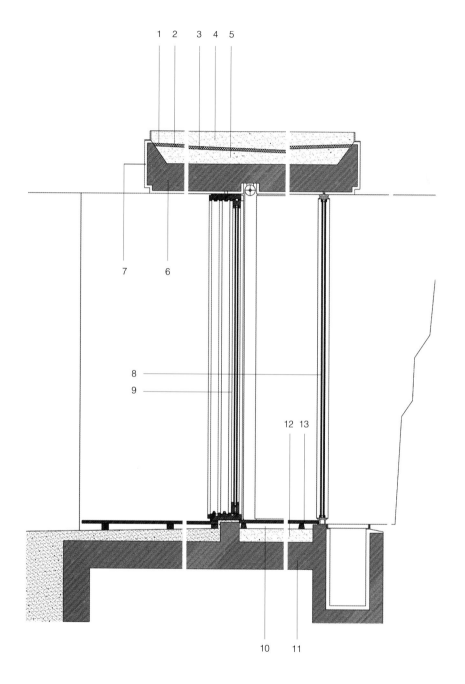

Detail drawing
1. Draining membrane
2. Thermal insulation
3. Waterproof membrane
4. Concrete screed levelling
5. Screed
6. Concrete slab
7. Plaster
8. Stainless steel casement
9. Wood casement
10. Underfloor heating system
11. Concrete slab
12. Screed
13. Timber floor

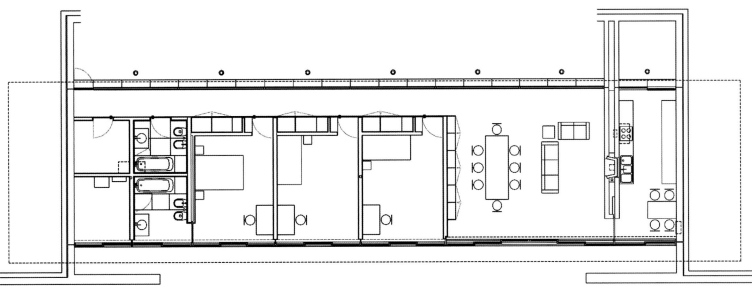

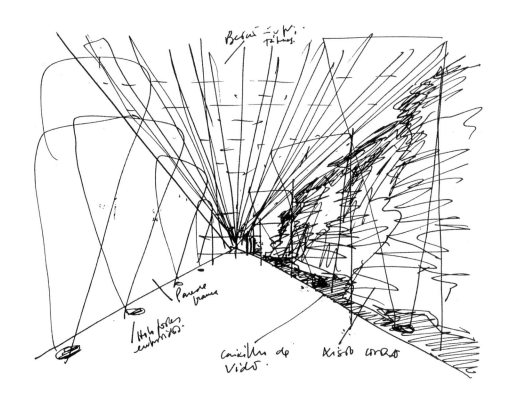

⑮ Courtyard Houses in Matosinhos

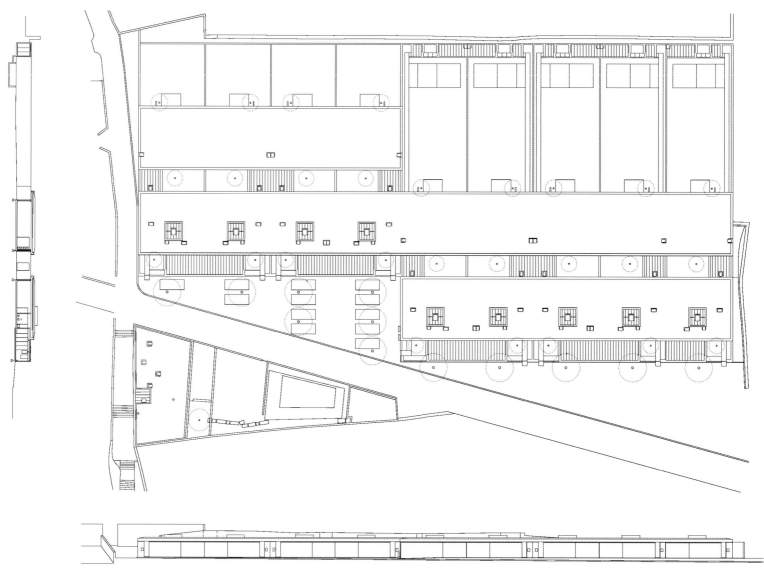

General plan

Project Year: 1993
Construction Year: 1999
Address: Rua Cartelas Vieira
Location: Matosinhos, Portugal
Client: Miguel Pereira Leite e Outros
Collaborators: Silvia Alves, Manuela Lara,
Filipe Pinto da Cruz, Teresa Gonçalves, Laura Peretti
Structural Consultants: G.O.P.
Electrical Consultants: Eng°. Raul Serafim
General Contractor: Comporto
Photographer: Luís Ferreira Alves
Building Size: 3,033 m^2
Lot Size: 7,340 m^2

An aristocratic villa with a beautiful garden had been sold and was being used as a venue for wedding celebrations. The house's vegetable garden, running parallel to Porto de Leixões, was sold off as plots for development. A new road, proposed by the local authority, was to cut diagonally across the vegetable garden to leave a triangle (one plot) and a trapezium (nine plots). The project sets out to occupy the trapezium, dividing it into four small and five large plots, with swimming pools and annexes. The plots are separated by parallel walls, which support three strips of concrete which act as roofs. The spaces between the walls are courtyards, where the vegetation will grow up above the walls to merge with the neighbouring gardens and fields. I believe that the place, laid out with walls and trees, will retain its identity.

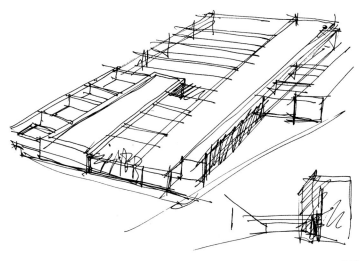

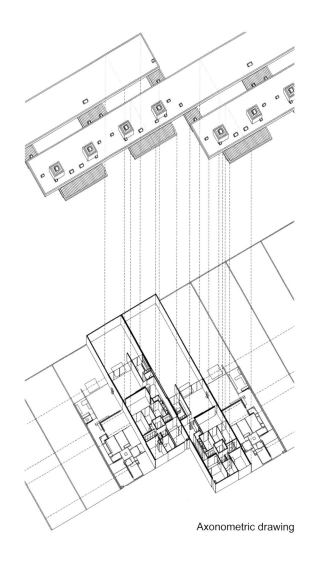

Axonometric drawing

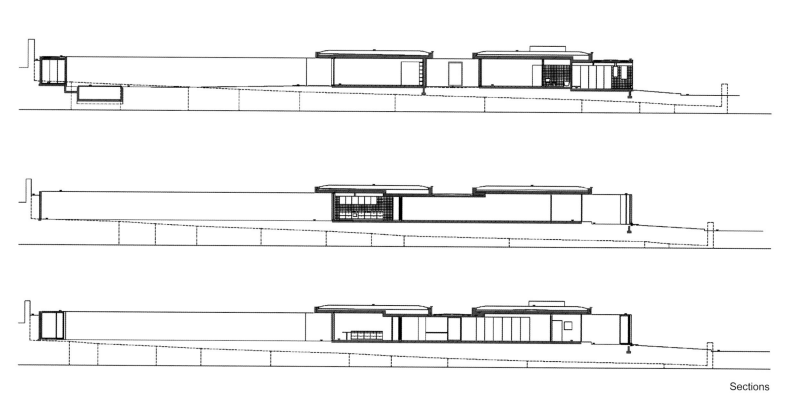

Sections

Plan (Below)
1. Entrance
2. Hall / Study
3. Garage
4. Dressing room
5. Bedroom
6. Kitchen
7. Living room
8. Swimming pool
9. Laundry
10. Courtyard
11. Storage
12. Restroom

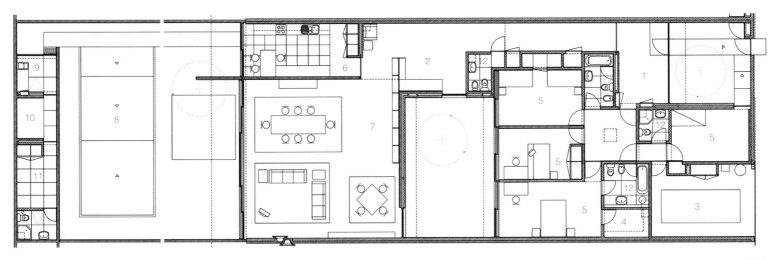

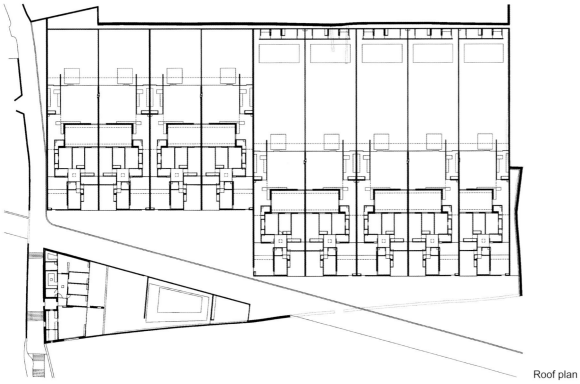

Roof plan

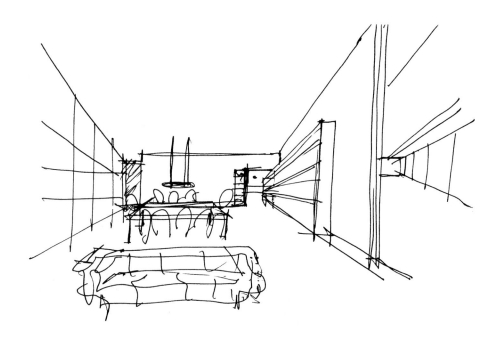

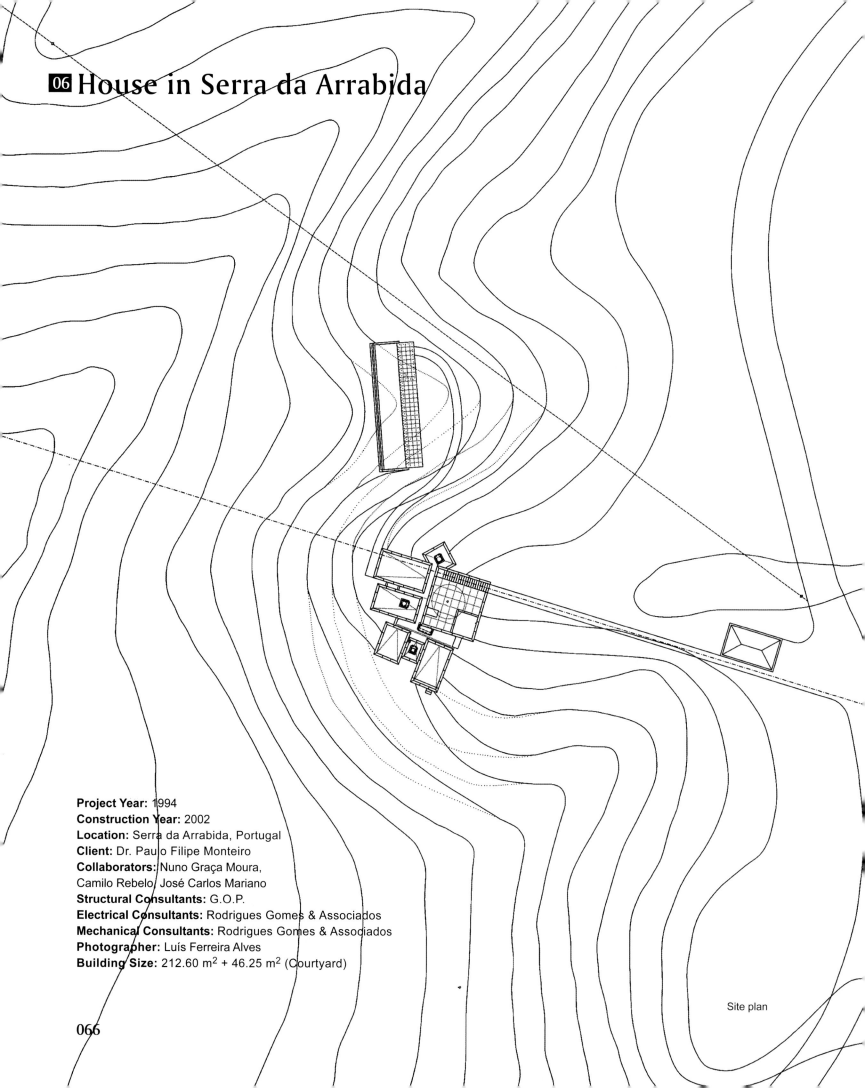

06 House in Serra da Arrabida

Project Year: 1994
Construction Year: 2002
Location: Serra da Arrabida, Portugal
Client: Dr. Paulo Filipe Monteiro
Collaborators: Nuno Graça Moura,
Camilo Rebelo, José Carlos Mariano
Structural Consultants: G.O.P.
Electrical Consultants: Rodrigues Gomes & Associados
Mechanical Consultants: Rodrigues Gomes & Associados
Photographer: Luís Ferreira Alves
Building Size: 212.60 m² + 46.25 m² (Courtyard)

Site plan

The project for the Arrabida House has been in progress for almost four years and I have only now obtained the building permit from the local authority. At the present moment I have passed beyond the permanent crisis, the personal difficulties with the definition of the language, and the final construction project is ready to go ahead. One of the problems was the incompatibility, with regard to the client, the topography and to me, of reconciling any previous experience with this project. The simple solutions were exhausted, and quickly became simplistic. The form transformed itself into formula. A text by the writer Edgar Morin serves to explain the situation: "In the face of increasing complexity, we are more than ever in need of a thought that is capable of simplifying without mutilating. When reality resists simplification, we have to turn to complexity. Complexity is the eruption of the disorder of the aleatory and of uncertainty into reality... We all know today that the future is unpredictable, given the perpetual intervention of the new and the unexpected. And it is for that very reason that extreme complexity has a tendency to resemble a permanent crisis." (Edgar Morin, "*O Jornal*" 24th December, 1986)

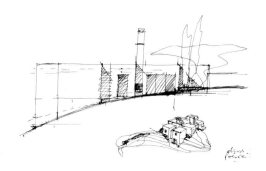

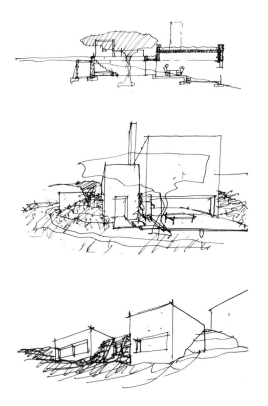

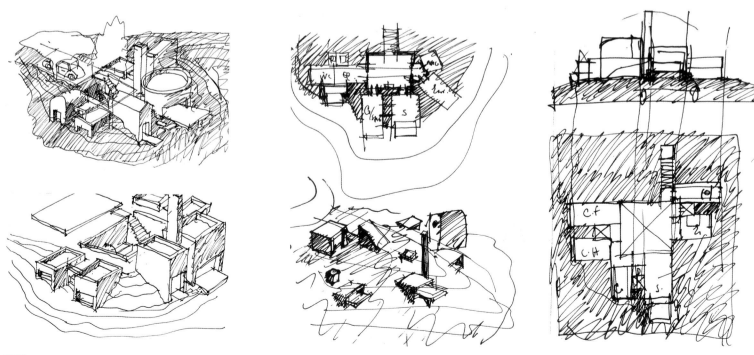

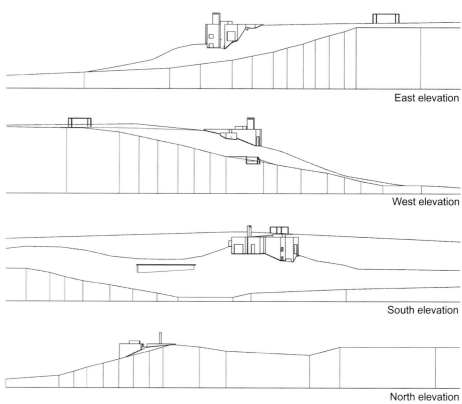

East elevation

West elevation

South elevation

North elevation

071

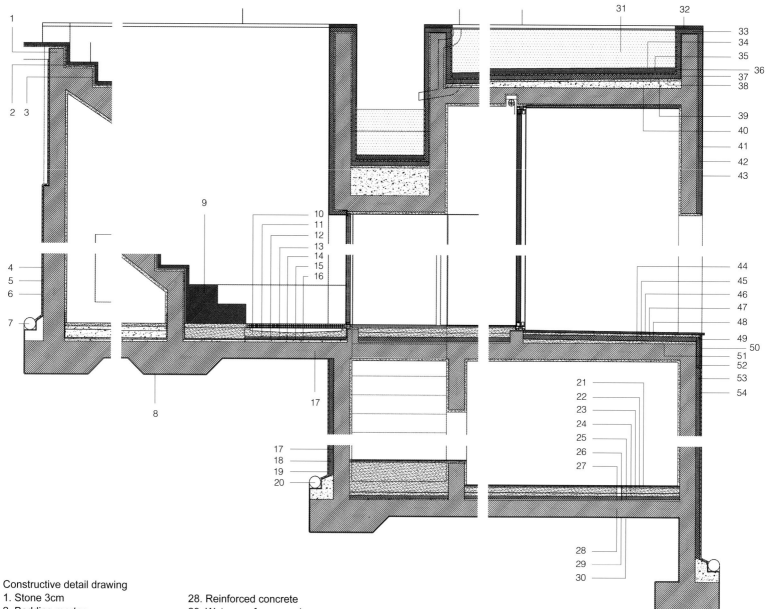

Constructive detail drawing

1. Stone 3cm
2. Bedding mortar
3. Regularisation
4. Enkadrain
5. Waterproof geomembrane
6. Geotextile
7. Drain
8. Waterproof geomembrane
9. Stone
10. Form layer
11. Geotextile
12. Roofmate isolation material 2cm
13. Sikaplan PVC screen
14. Geotextile
15. Regularisation
16. Screed
17. Waterproof geomembrane
18. Wallmate isolation material 40mm
19. Enkadrain
20. Drain
21. Marble
22. Bedding mortar
23. Screed
24. Screed armed
25. Polyethylene film
26. Roofmate isolation material 30mm
27. Regularisation

28. Reinforced concrete
29. Waterproof geomembrane
30. Tout-venant
31. Humus
32. Stone
33. Roofmate isolation material
34. Geotextile
35. Goth
36. Enkadrain
37. Roofmate isolation material 40mm
38. Sikaplan PVC geotextile screen
39. Floor screed materials
40. Lightweight concrete with a 1% drop
41. Cerezite
42. Wallmate isolation material 40mm
43. Reinforced plaster
44. Stone
45. Bedding mortar
46. Geotextile
47. Roofmate isolation material 40mm
48. PVC screen
49. Wallmate isolation material 20mm
50. Stone
51. Lightweight concrete with a 1% drop
52. Waterproof geomembrane
53. Wallmate isolation material 40mm
54. Enkadrain

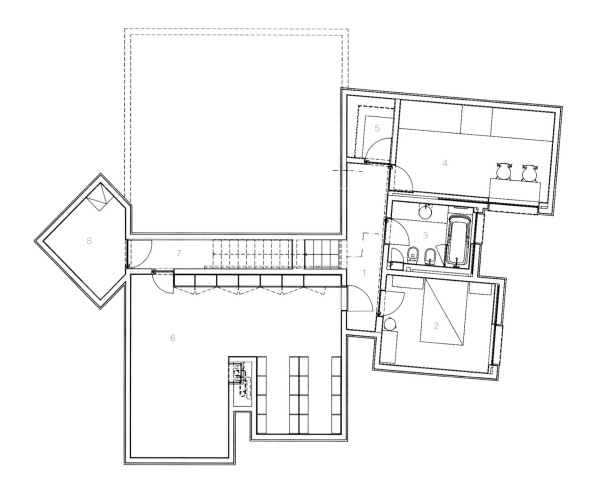

Ground floor plan
1. Hall
2. Room
3. Toilet
4. Room
5. Dressing room
6. Storage
7. Storage
8. Technical area

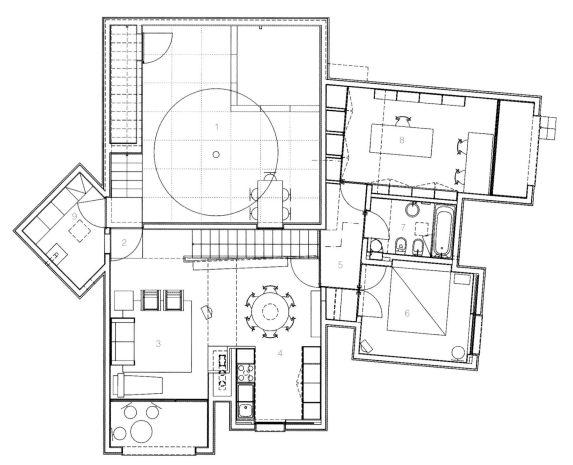

Basement floor plan
1. Patio
2. Entrance
3. Living room
4. Kitchen
5. Hall
6. Room
7. Toilet
8. Office
9. Laundry

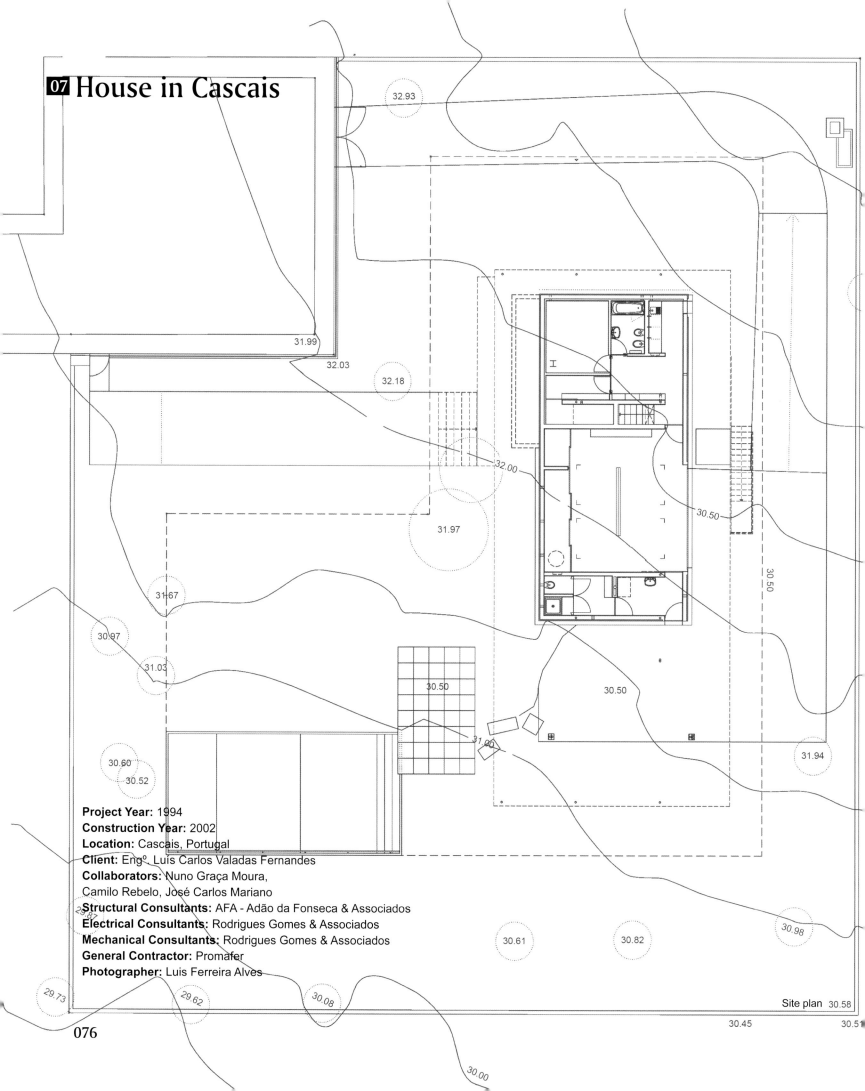

House in Cascais

31.99

32.03

32.93

32.18

32.00

31.97

30.50

30.50

31.67

30.97

31.03

30.50

30.50

31.94

30.60

30.52

31.00

Project Year: 1994
Construction Year: 2002
Location: Cascais, Portugal
Client: Eng°. Luís Carlos Valadas Fernandes
Collaborators: Nuno Graça Moura,
Camilo Rebelo, José Carlos Mariano
Structural Consultants: AFA - Adão da Fonseca & Associados
Electrical Consultants: Rodrigues Gomes & Associados
Mechanical Consultants: Rodrigues Gomes & Associados
General Contractor: Promafer
Photographer: Luis Ferreira Alves

29.87

30.61

30.82

30.98

29.73

29.62

30.08

Site plan 30.58

30.00

30.45

30.51

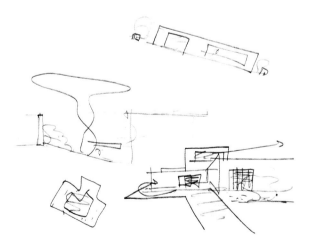

When designing a house, the problem is to understand the identity of both the client and the place in order to invent an "alter ego". Our capacity for repetition depends on our attitudes to the "time" and on the personality of the "place". I became interested in doors and windows, which I had felt inhibited about for 25 years. An immense horizontal sea, the Atlantic, cannot be recorded: an ocean - always different, always the same - cannot be "caught". We therefore opened up a neutral view, expanding the voids and designing with positives and negatives. The materials and colours are all different, all the same: grey. The grey tones vary gradually from outside to inside. The greys of Azulino de Cascais stone, the matt sheen of the aluminium and the sand-blasted stainless steel are all waiting for the setting sun to lift them out of their "grey" state.

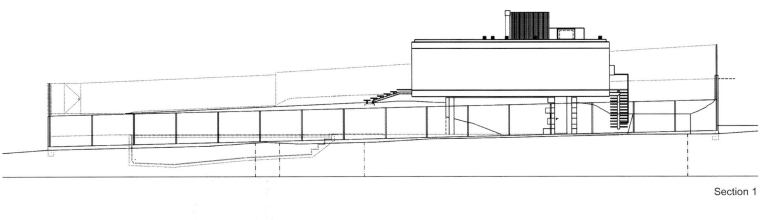

Section 1

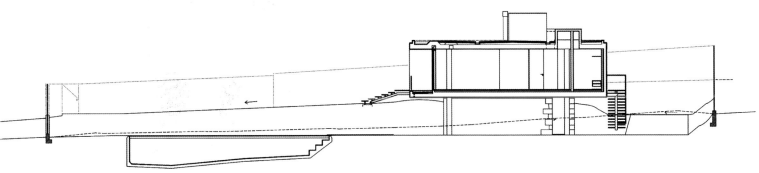

Section 2

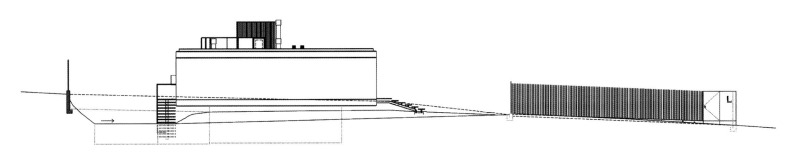

Section 3

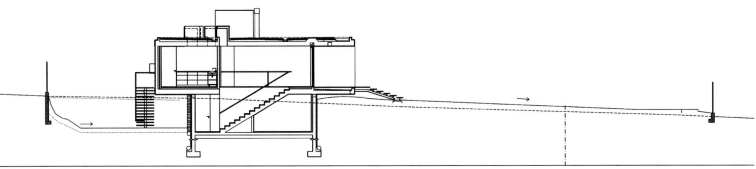

Section 4

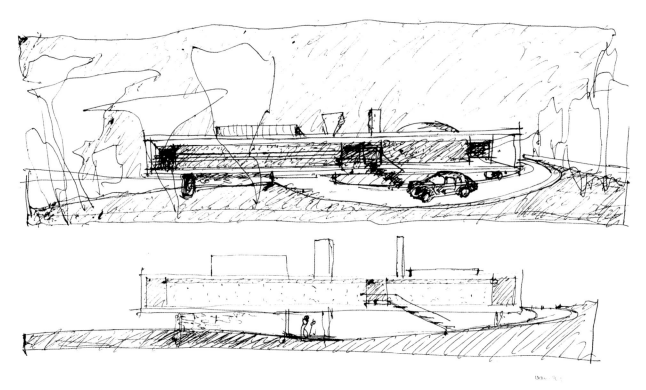

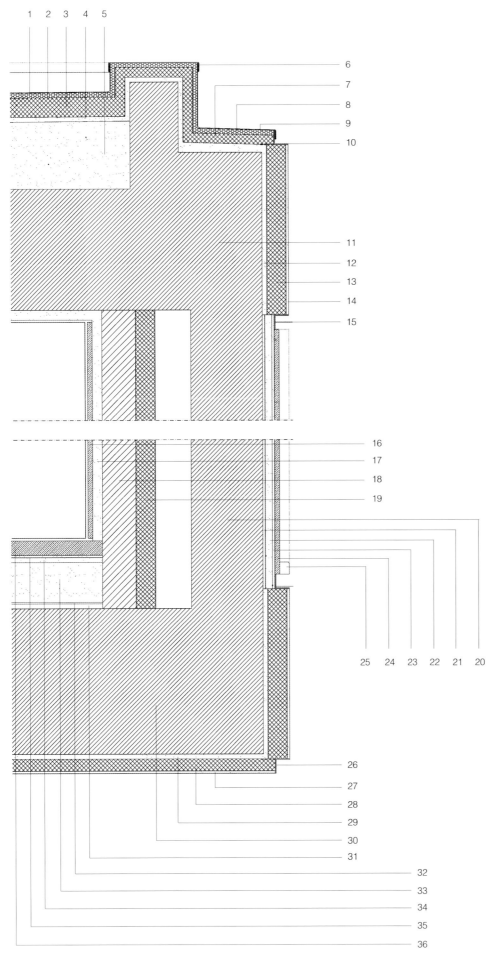

North façade (Kitchen) detail drawing
1. Camarinha type zinc plate
2. Delta MS Dörken
3. Roofmate isolation material 40mm
4. Regularisation (1cm)
5. Form layer (Lightweight concrete)
6. Zinc ruff
7. Roofmate isolation material 20mm
8. Delta MS Dörken
9. Zinc plate
10. Stainless steel corner 30x30x2mm
11. Concrete
12. Waterproof mortar
13. Expanded polystyrene 40mm
14. Dryvit type armed and colored concrete
15. Stainless steel corner 30x30x2mm
16. Handmade tile 14x14cm
17. Regularisation/Settlement
18. Waterproof mortar
19. Wallmate isolation material 40mm
20. Concrete
21. Waterproof mortar
22. Regularisation
23. Bedding mortar
24. Handmade tile 14x14cm
25. Marble threshold
26. Stainless steel corner 30x30x2 mm
27. Dryvit type armed and coloured concrete
28. Expanded polystyrene 25mm
29. Waterproof mortar
30. Concrete slab
31. Regularisation
32. Acoustic screen
33. Filling
34. Regularisation
35. Bedding mortar
36. Marble

083

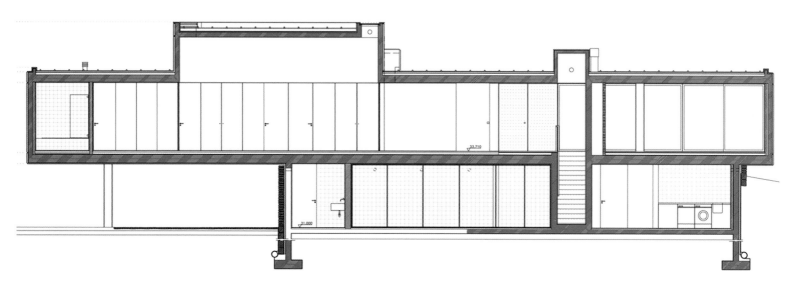

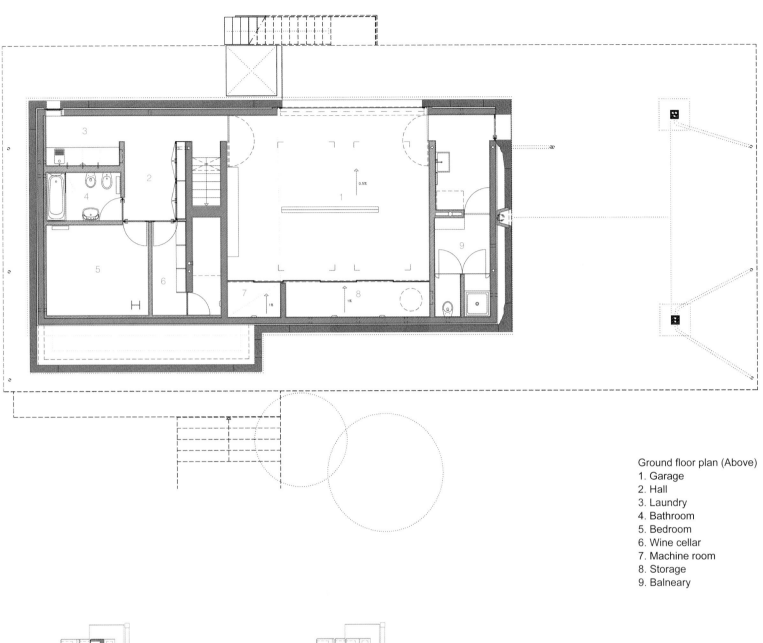

Ground floor plan (Above)
1. Garage
2. Hall
3. Laundry
4. Bathroom
5. Bedroom
6. Wine cellar
7. Machine room
8. Storage
9. Balneary

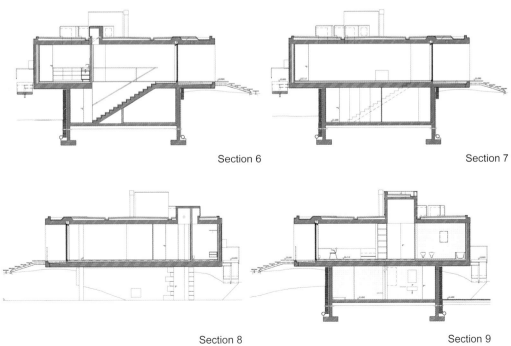

Section 6

Section 7

Section 8

Section 9

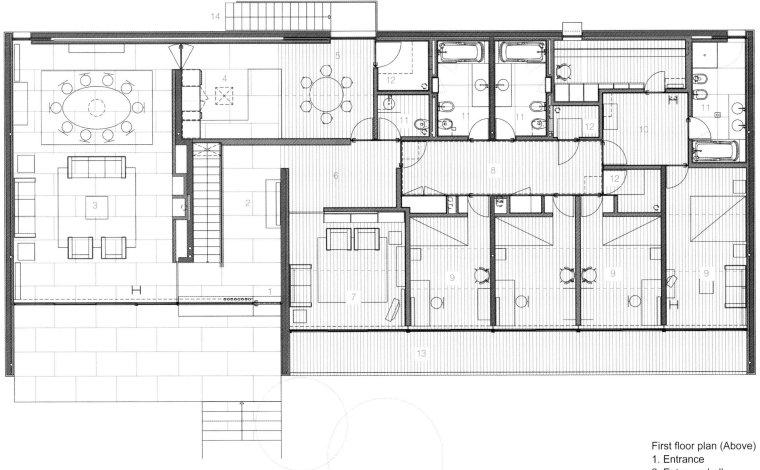

First floor plan (Above)
1. Entrance
2. Entrance hall
3. Living room
4. Kitchen
5. Pantry
6. Hall
7. Television room
8. Corridor
9. Bedroom
10. Hall (Suite)
11. Restrooms
12. Dressing room
13. Balcony
14. Stairs

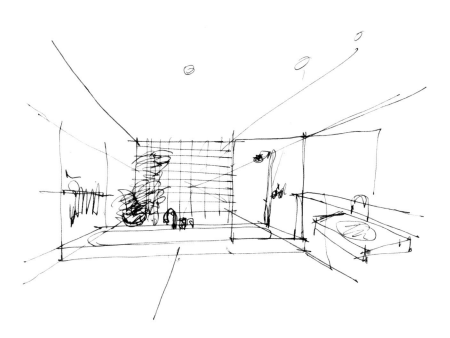

087

08 House in "Bom Jesus" II

Project Year: 1996-2004
Construction Year: 2004-2007
Address: Lamaçães
Location: Bom Jesus, Braga, Portugal
Client: Dr. Fernando Vaz
Collaborators: Susana Meirinhos, Luís Peixoto, Tomás Neves
Structural Consultants: S.G.P.E.
Electrical Consultants: Fernando Ramos
Mechanical Consultants: Matos Campos
General Contractor: Sá Machado & Filhos
Photographer: Luís Ferreira Alves
Building Size: 1,171 m²
Lot Size: 5,050 m²

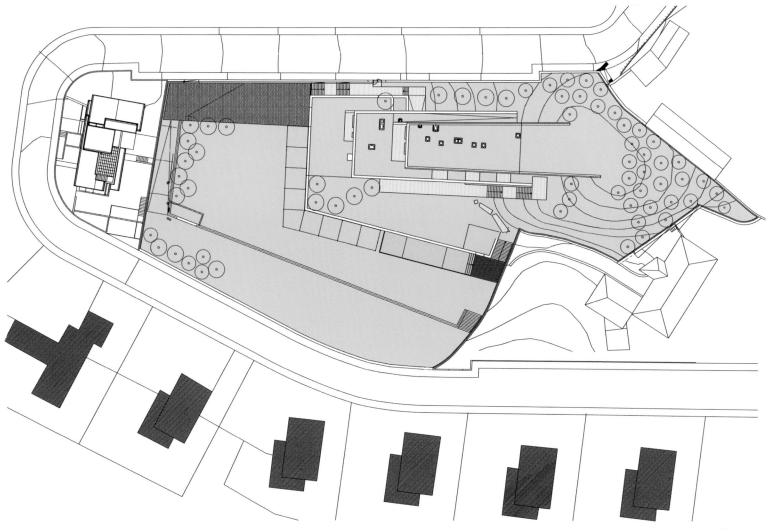

Site plan

To meet the client's requirements we designed a black and white house with large terraces overlooking the city. The image of the *Art House Project in Naoshima - Minami Dera Temple* by Tadao Ando came up as an excuse for the black and also because the client was a timber industrial. Because the site was a fairly steep hill overlooking the city of Braga, we decided not to produce a large volume resting on a hilltop. The house was to be a wooden box but due to maintenance issues it will now be coated with patinaed zinc. Instead, we made the construction on five terraces with retainer walls, with a different function defined for each terrace - fruit trees on the lowest level, a swimming pool on the next, the main parts of the house on the next, bedrooms on the fourth, and on the top, we planted a forest. Those terraces' drawings led us to involve the house in a heroically suspended ring. The ring will probably be painted in white. Between this ring and the house a garden embraces the vertical oak-trees. On the house's south and west sides the terraces' horizontal subbase planes could be aligned with the skyline. (Porto, August 2009, Eduardo Souto de Moura)

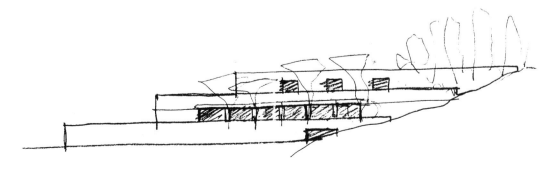

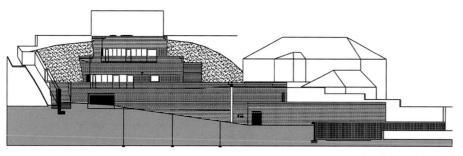

Southeast elevation

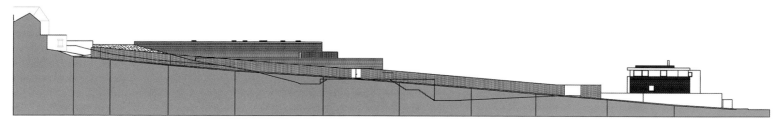

Northeast elevation (Section 1)

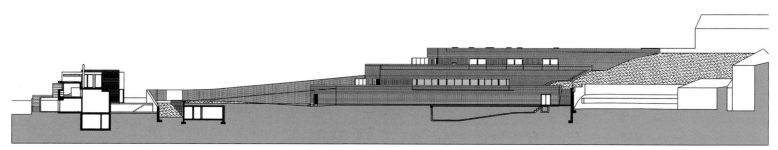

Southwest elevation (Section 2)

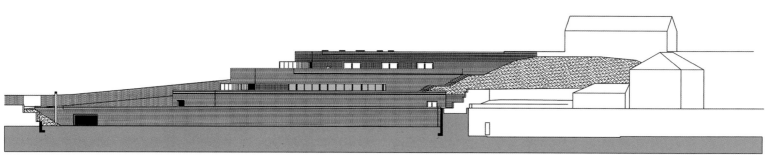

Southwest elevation (Section 3)

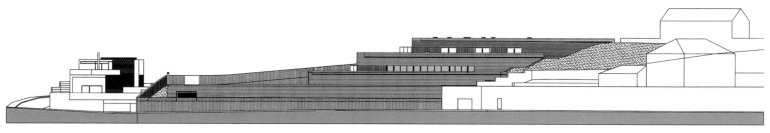

Southwest elevation (Section 4)

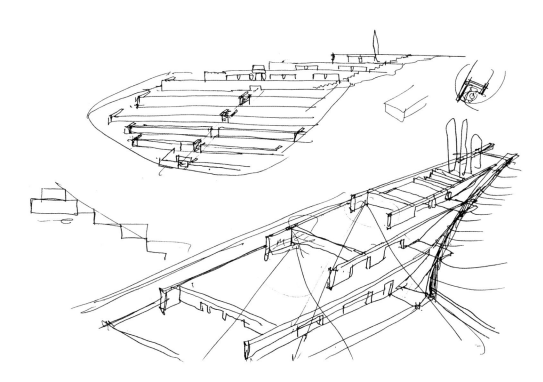

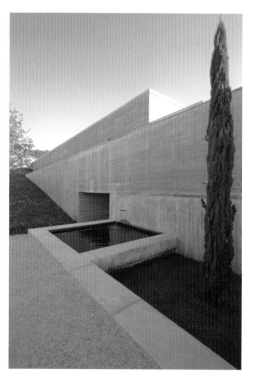

Detail section drawing
1. "Wavin" drain omega ¢ 100 mm
2. Grass
3. Sand substrate 4cm
4. Fine sand 13cm
5. Thick area 10cm
6. LECA 20cm
7. "Cordrain" 16mm
8. Alkorplan L membrane 35177 (1.5mm)
9. Alkorplus protection layer 81005 (300g/m^2)
10. Roofmate isolation material 40mm
11. Alkorplus vapour control layer 81012
12. Form layer with regularisation and 1% drop
13. Wooden floor
14. Wood slats
15. Armed screed
16. Floormate isolation material 30mm
17. Regularisation
18. Concrete slab
19. Waterproof geomembrane
20. Sub-foundation of tout-venant
21. Support structure of the plasterboard
22. Waterproof plasterboard 15mm
23. Concrete wall 20cm
24. Screed 8cm with 1% drop
25. Concrete screed
26. Rockfill

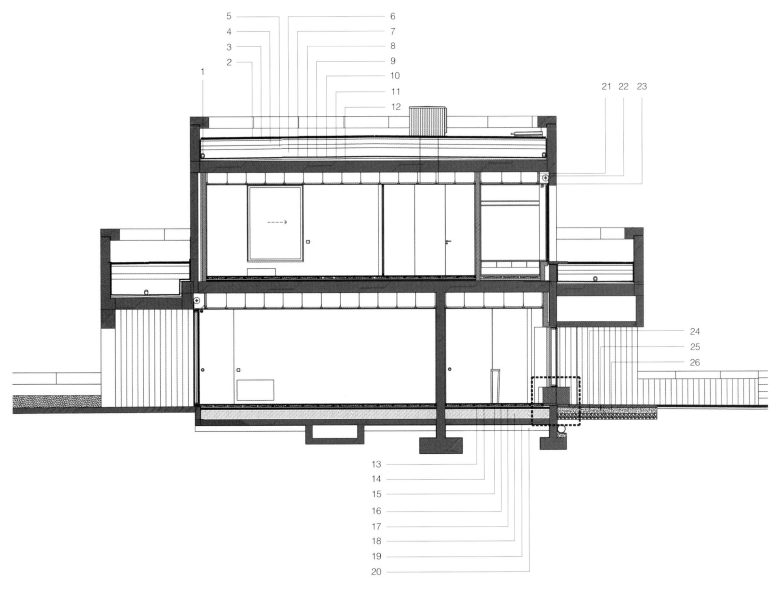

093

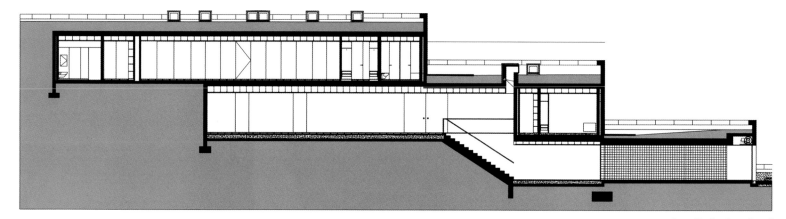

Longitudinal section 1

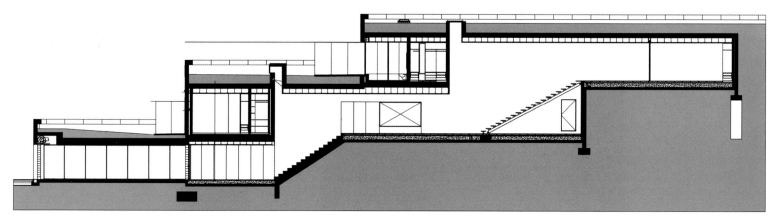

Longitudinal section 2

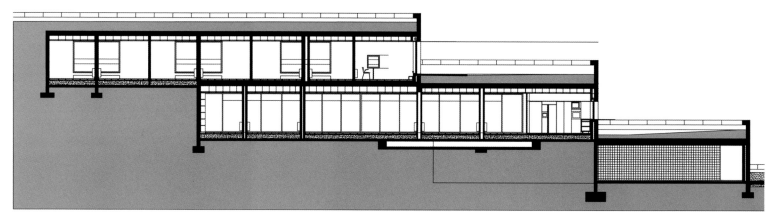

Longitudinal section 3

Cave plan (Right)
1. Garage
2. Tidy room
3. Technical area
4. Hall
5. Restroom
6. Storage
7. Kitchen
8. Swimming pool
9. Vestibule / kitchenette
10. Technical area / tidy room of chairs
11. Spa

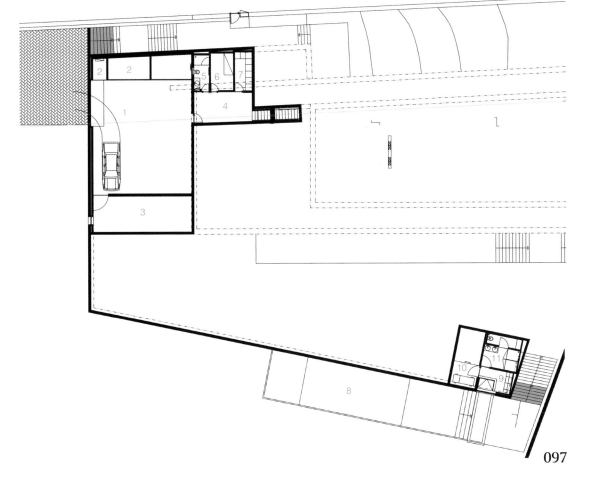

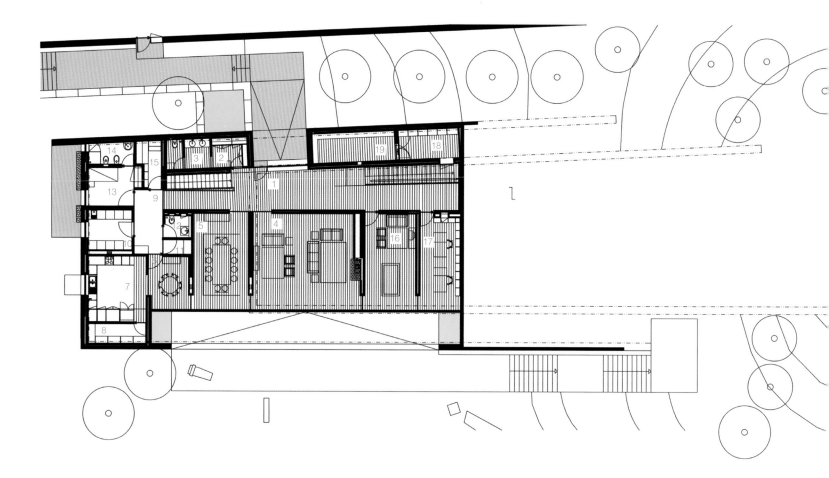

Ground floor plan (Above) 10. Laundry
1. Hall   11. Service room
2. Cloakroom   12. Storage
3. Service room   13. Service room
4. Living room   14. Restroom
5. Dining room   15. Storage
6. Breakfast room   16. Playroom
7. Kitchen   17. Office
8. Pantry   18. Storage
9. Service hall   19. Vault

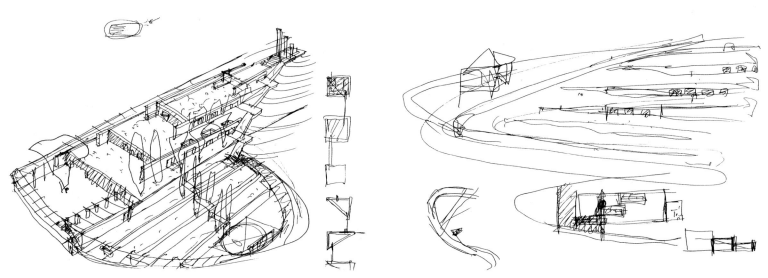

Project Year: 1996
Construction Year: 2005-2007
Address: Rua Nicolau Nasoni, Lotes 1 e 9
Location: Maia, Portugal
Client: Fernando Dias
Collaborators: Luís Peixoto, Susana Meirinhos
Structural Consultants: AFA consult - Engº Rui Furtado,
Engº Miguel Paula Rocha
Electrical Consultants: AFA consult - Engº Raul Serafim
Mechanical Consultants: AFA consult - Engª Isabel Sarmento
Hydraulic: AFA consult - Engº Paulo Silva
Landscaping: Engº Manuel Pedro Melo
Constructor: Matriz
Photographer: Luís Ferreira Alves

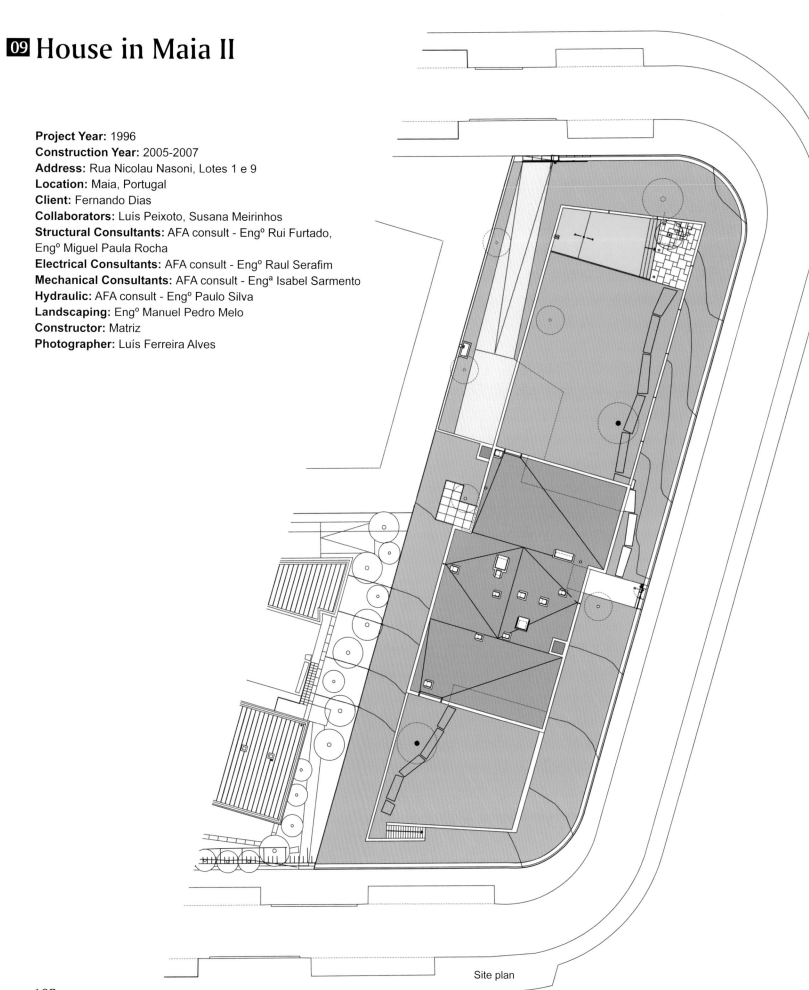

Site plan

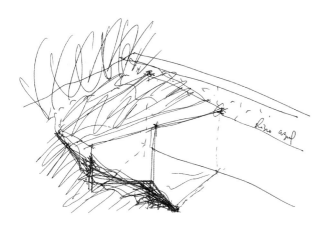

The house is developed on two lots whose ends have a height of seven metres. Moving forward to the middle between two volumes, the programme looks like this: the rooms on the east, and the living room as well as others on the west. Below, is a basement with a porch that serves as a garage, pool and the engine room. The house has two patios and gardens with two different geographies: to the east, the rooms, a more intimate area with a tranquil oriental garden that provides the necessary light; to the west lies a long garden with oaks on the north, falling into a pool where a window lets you see the industrial outskirts and subway passes.

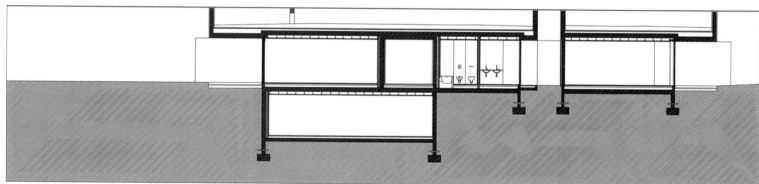

Section 1

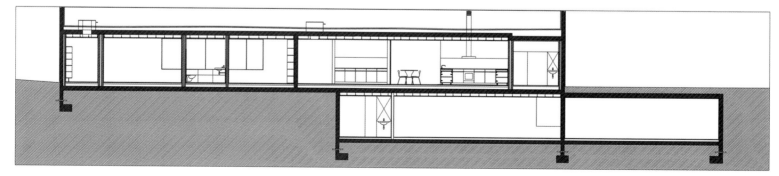

Section 2

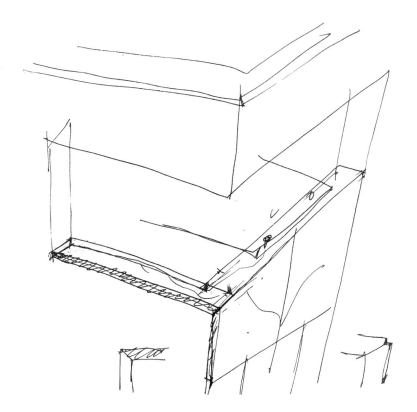

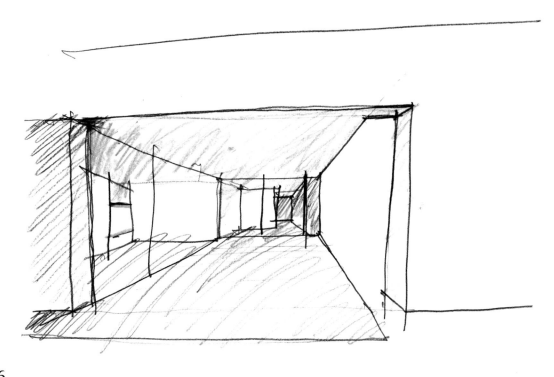

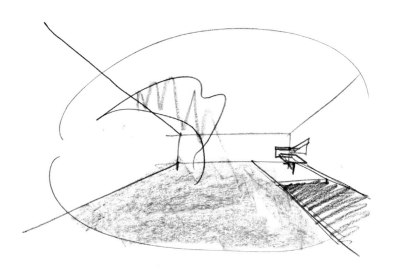
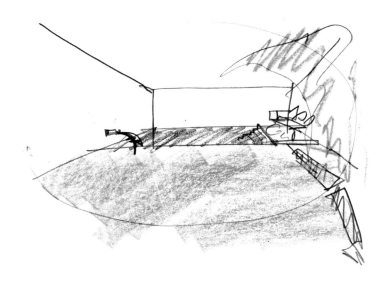

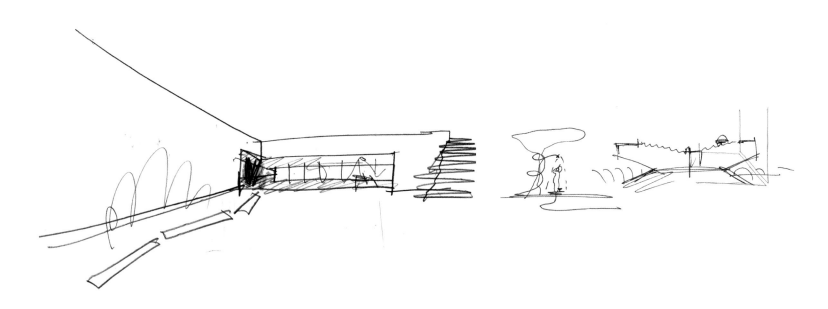

Ground floor plan (Below)
1. Hall / entrance
2. Room 1
3. Corridor 1
4. Hall
5. Corridor 2
6. Hall 2
7. Hall 3
8. Patio
9. Bedroom suite
10. Bedroom 2
11. Bedroom 3
12. Hall 4
13. Bedroom 4
14. Room 2
15. Pantry
16. Laundry
17. Kitchen
18. Dining room

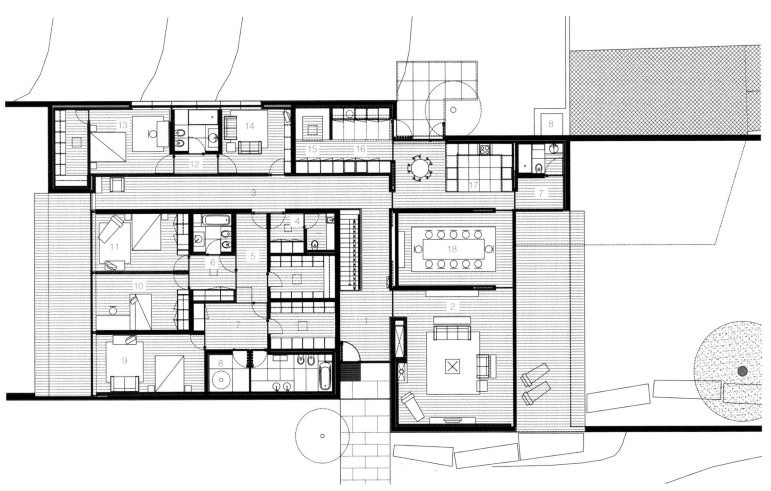

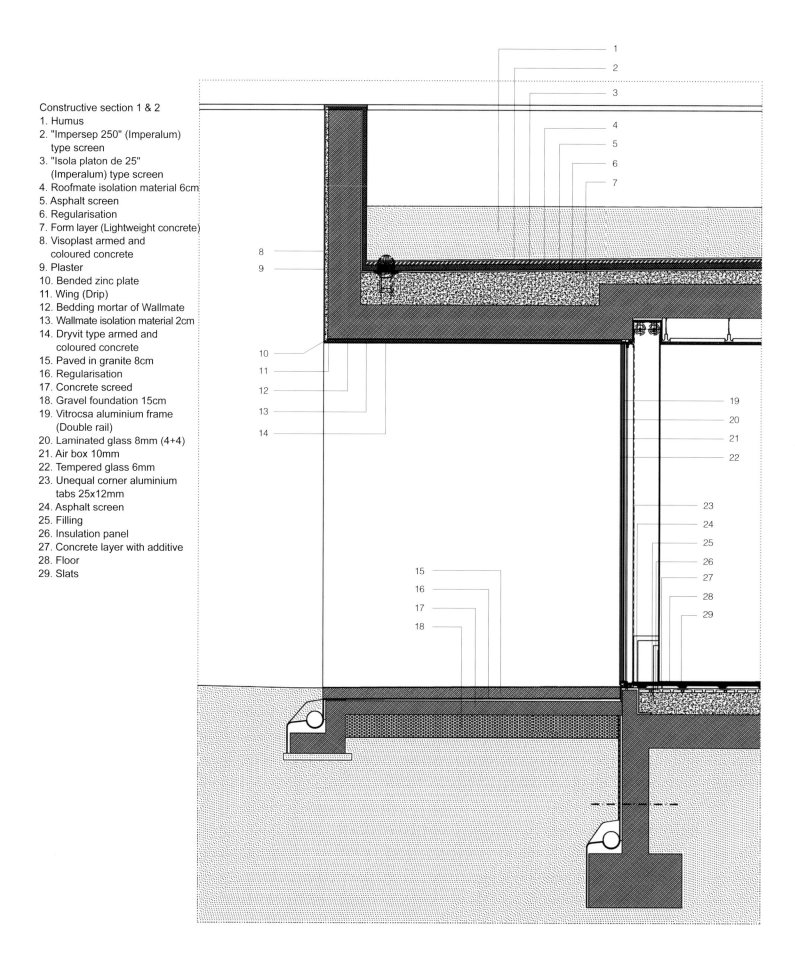

Constructive section 1 & 2
1. Humus
2. "Impersep 250" (Imperalum) type screen
3. "Isola platon de 25" (Imperalum) type screen
4. Roofmate isolation material 6cm
5. Asphalt screen
6. Regularisation
7. Form layer (Lightweight concrete)
8. Visoplast armed and coloured concrete
9. Plaster
10. Bended zinc plate
11. Wing (Drip)
12. Bedding mortar of Wallmate
13. Wallmate isolation material 2cm
14. Dryvit type armed and coloured concrete
15. Paved in granite 8cm
16. Regularisation
17. Concrete screed
18. Gravel foundation 15cm
19. Vitrocsa aluminium frame (Double rail)
20. Laminated glass 8mm (4+4)
21. Air box 10mm
22. Tempered glass 6mm
23. Unequal corner aluminium tabs 25x12mm
24. Asphalt screen
25. Filling
26. Insulation panel
27. Concrete layer with additive
28. Floor
29. Slats

114

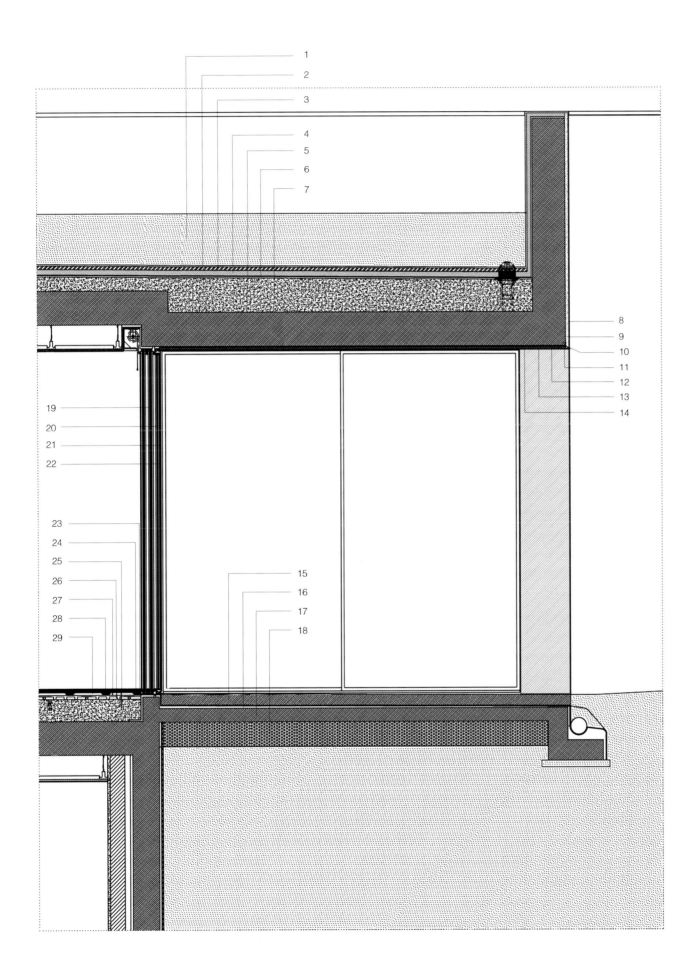

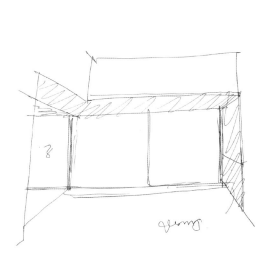

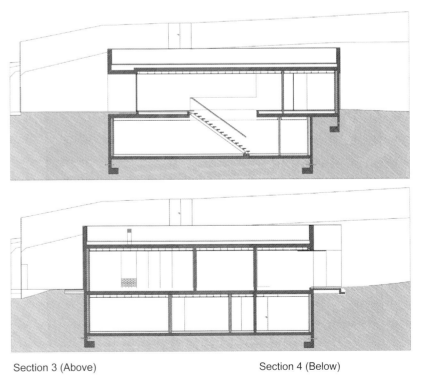

Section 3 (Above)

Section 4 (Below)

117

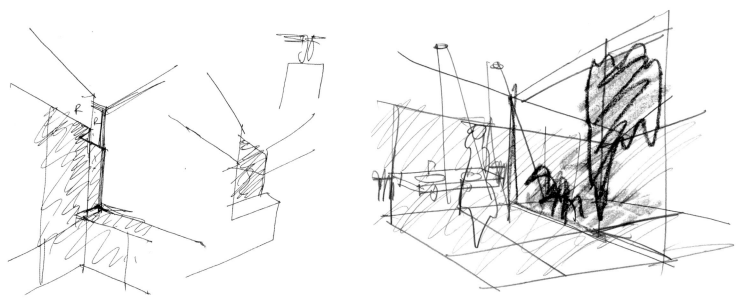

⑩ Commercial Building in Maia City

Project Year: 1997
Construction Year: 1998-2001
Address: Rua Clotilde Ferreira da Cruz - E.N.14
Location: Maia, Portugal
Client: Sr. Ribeiro
Collaborators: Tomás Neves, José Carlos Mariano
Structural Consultants: Enarte - Engenharia e Arquitectura, Lda.
Electrical Consultants: Enarte - Engenharia e Arquitectura, Lda.
Mechanical Consultants: Enarte - Engenharia e Arquitectura, Lda.
Landscape Design: Laura Costa
General Contractor: Ribeiro de Sousa & Silva Correia, Lda.
Photographer: Luís Ferreira Alves
Building Size: 6,412.2 m²
Cost: 4,588,940.65 Euros

The building is designed for collective housing and has 32 flats and 8 commercial spaces. The construction area is 45 metres x 17 metres with a ground floor and five storeys. The rectangle was divided through its axis creating two separate bodies which are continuous and symmetric, yet independent in terms of accesses and entrances. The lifts, staircases, bathrooms, storage areas and service areas compose the building's central structure, allowing better interior organisation. The eastern elevation includes two entrances, four of the commercial entrances and the car entrances for the basements car park. The western façade gives direct access to four commercial spaces. The flat typology has the kitchen near the entrance, next to the living room and the bedrooms creating a linear front, structured by a corridor with 1.40 metres wide. The structure metric is based on a square, 5.9 metres large, creating bedroom fronts of 2.95 metres and parking spaces of the same size. The wall openings define the façade modulation which is a system of aluminium venetian blinds. This system has two types: the first, fixed to the exterior wall and the second, a normal blind for the windows and the laundry openings. This principle stands on the ground floor in the commercial spaces. The window frames are made of aluminium in its natural colour. The flat floor is made of wood boards, and the walls are covered with plaster or clay tiles in the bathrooms.

North elevation

South elevation

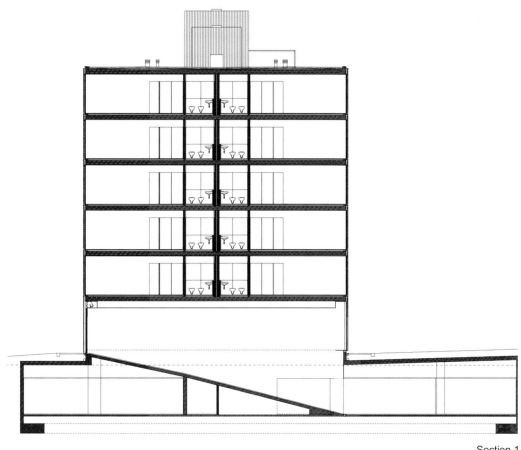

Section 1

123

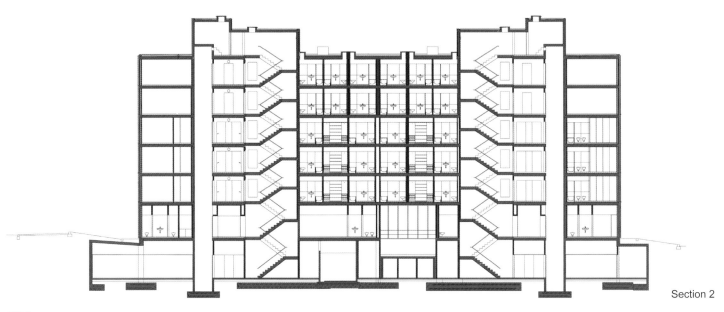

Section 2

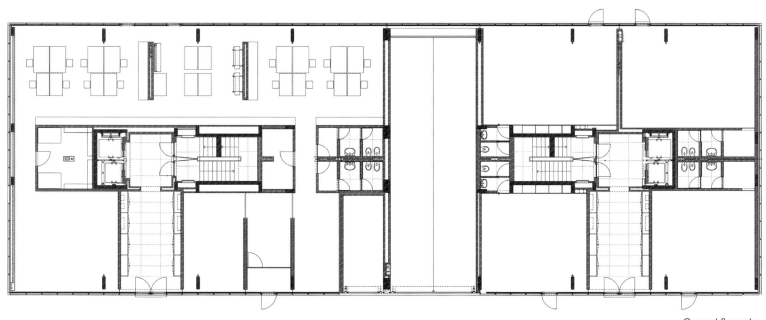

Ground floor plan

Vertical section version
1. Brick wall 0.11
2. Waterproof regularisation
3. Wallmate isolation material 3cm
4. Guide rail of the blind
5. Asphalt screen
6. U-shape stainless steel for lashing the sill
   with 0.30 separation
7. Sill in bended aluminium plate 3.5mm
8. Support brackets to the rails
9. Rail of the blind roller
10. Blades of the blind
11. Concrete slab
12. Waterproof regularisation
13. Wallmate isolation material 4cm
14. Guide rail of the blind
15. Aluminium corner 40x40x4mm
16. Brick wall 0.11
17. Waterproof regularisation
18. Wallmate isolation material 3cm
19. Guide rail of the blind
20. Asphalt screen
21. U-shape stainless steel for lashing
    the sill with 0.50 separation
22. Sill in bended aluminium plate 3.5mm
23. Support brackets to the rails
24. Rail of the blind roller
25. Blades of the blind
26. Concrete slab
27. Waterproof regularisation
28. Wallmate isolation material 4cm
29. Guide rail of the blind
30. Brick wall 0.11
31. Plaster tin
32. Wing
33. Hardwood parquet
34. Glue of settlement
35. Regularisation of armed screed
36. Isolphone type acoustic screen
37. Form layer of cork concrete
38. Concrete slab
39. Plaster stucco
40. Wing
41. Brick wall 0.11
42. Plaster tin
43. Wing
44. Hardwood parquet
45. Glue of settlement
46. Regularisation of armed screed
47. Isolphone type acoustic screen
48. Form layer of cork concrete
49. Concrete slab

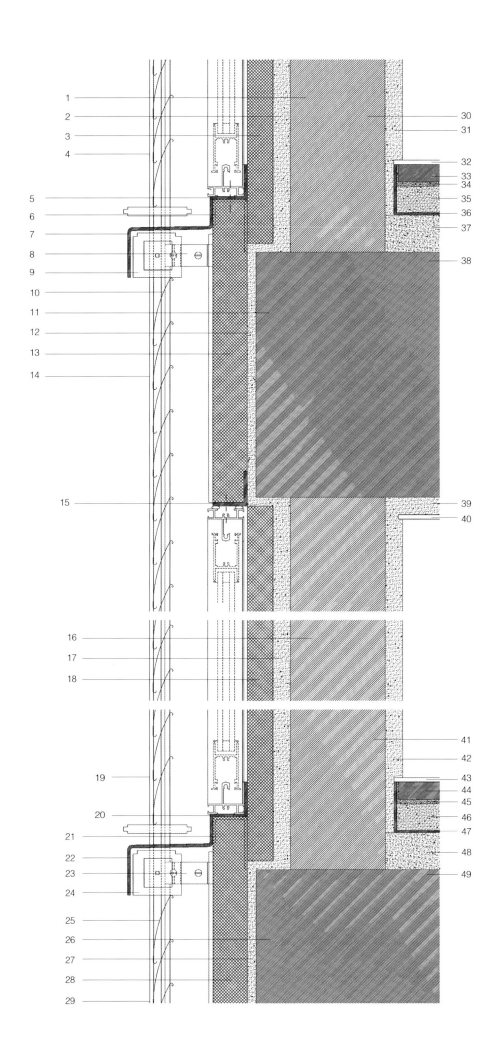

126

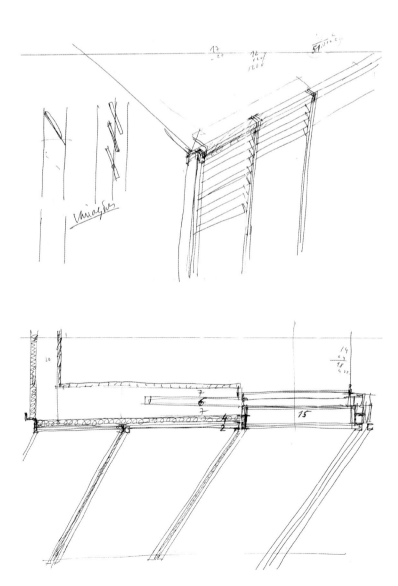

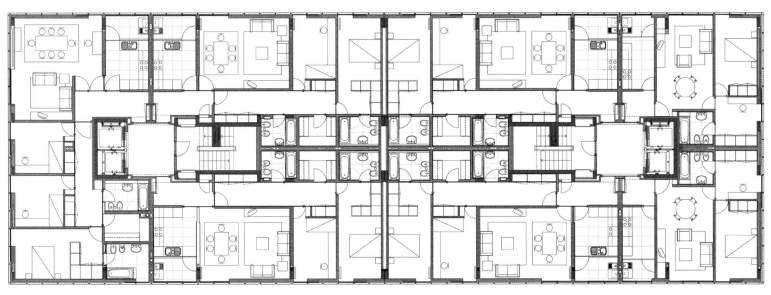

First floor plan

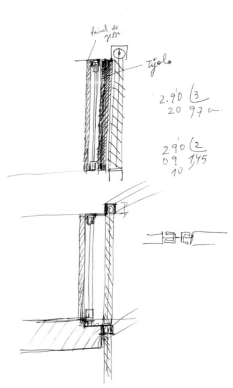

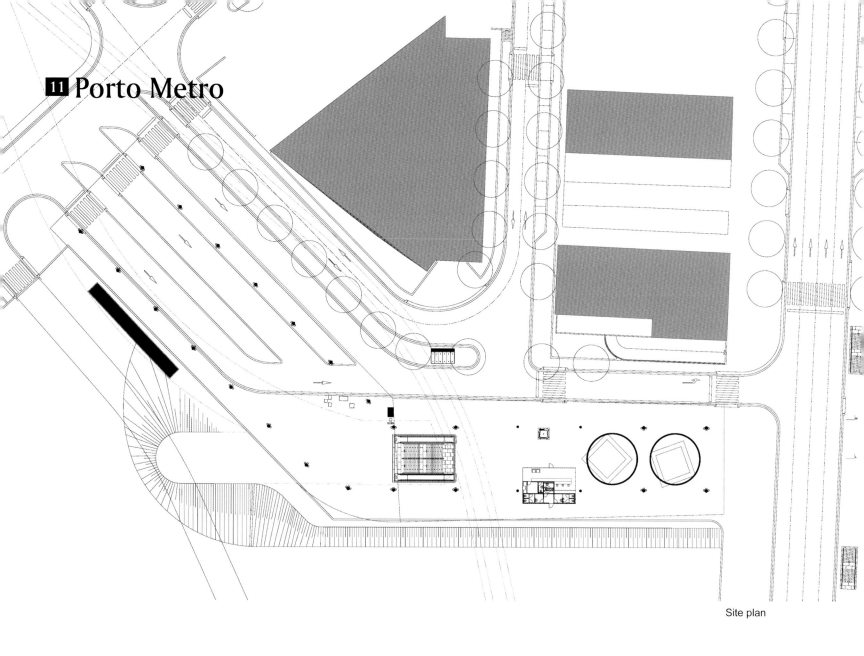

11 Porto Metro

Site plan

Project Year: 1997
Construction Year: 2005
Address: Porto
Location: Porto, Portugal
Client: Metro do Porto
Architectural Team:
Coordinator: Arq. Adriano Pimenta
Collaborators:
Arq. André Campos,
Arq. Ricardo Tedim, Arq. Eduardo Carrilho,
Arq. Joana Pinho, José Carlos Mariano,
Arq. Bernardo Durão, Arq. Diogo Crespo,
Arq. Manuel Pais Vieira, Arq. Nuno Flores,
Arq. Nuno Lopes, Arq. Tiago Coelho,
Arq. Tiago Figueiredo,
Aqr. Eduardo Pereira, Pedro Chimeno,
Soares da Costa - Gabinete de Projectos

Foundations and Structural Consultants:
CENOR - Projectos de Engenharia, Lda.
COBA - Consultores para Obras,
Barragens e Planeamento, S.A.
CJC - Engenharia e Projectos, Lda.
VIA PONTE - Projectos e Consultoria de Engenharia, Lda.
Hidraulic Consultant: FASE - Estudos e Projectos, S.A.
Construction Consortium: Normetro ACE
Civil Construction (Project + Execution):
Transmetro (Soares da Costa, Somague, Impregilo)
Power and Electrification: Balfour Beatty Rail
Rail Signalling System and Vehicles:
Bombardier Transportation
Management Operation and Maintenance: Transdev
Concept Engineering: Semaly
Photographer: Luís Ferreira Alves
Building Size: 60 km of railway and 69 Stations

132

The poet Pablo Neruda, when he was to receive the Nobel Prize, included in his speech of thanks a short quotation from Rimbaud, "...at dawn, armed with an ardent patience, we shall enter the splendid cities." When we go down the Av. República in the morning, coming from St. Ovídio, and cross the Luís I bridge, "...armed with an ardent patience, we shall enter the splendid cities, Porto". Initially it seemed almost impossible to make the rigorous technical specifications which determine the system compatible with the dramatic topography of the historic centre of the city. However, during the course of the project we became convinced of its feasibility. With the evolution of the project something that might have been an obstacle - a closed and unaccommodating system - was transformed into a factor for the redesign of the city. Minor changes in the levels of the streets and adjustments to the correspondence of slopes, pavements, gardens, trees, street furniture and lighting are some of the aspects of regrading that the surface metro line suggested and which the city needed and we could not put off for the future.

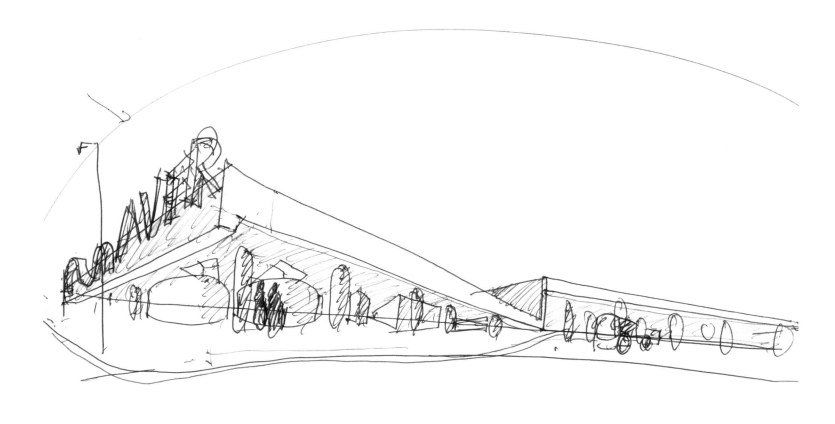

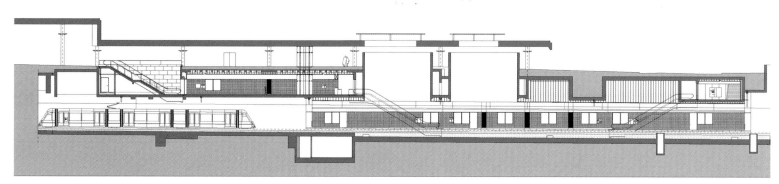

Section 1

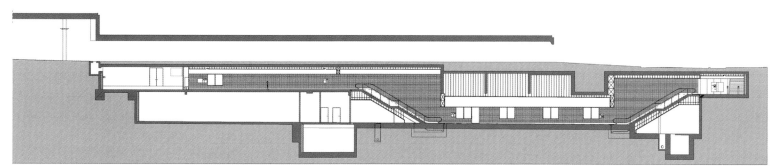

Section 2

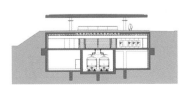  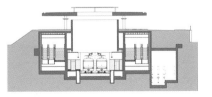 

Sections

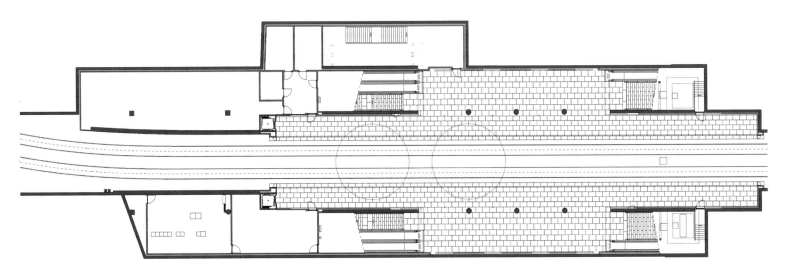

Platform level plan

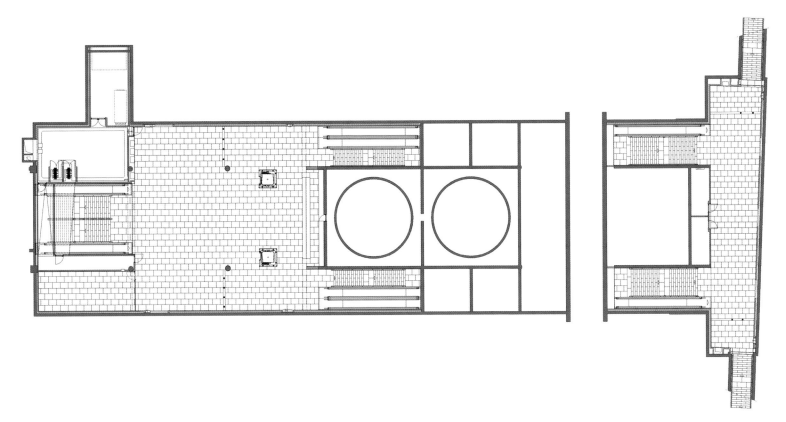

Atrium level plan

137

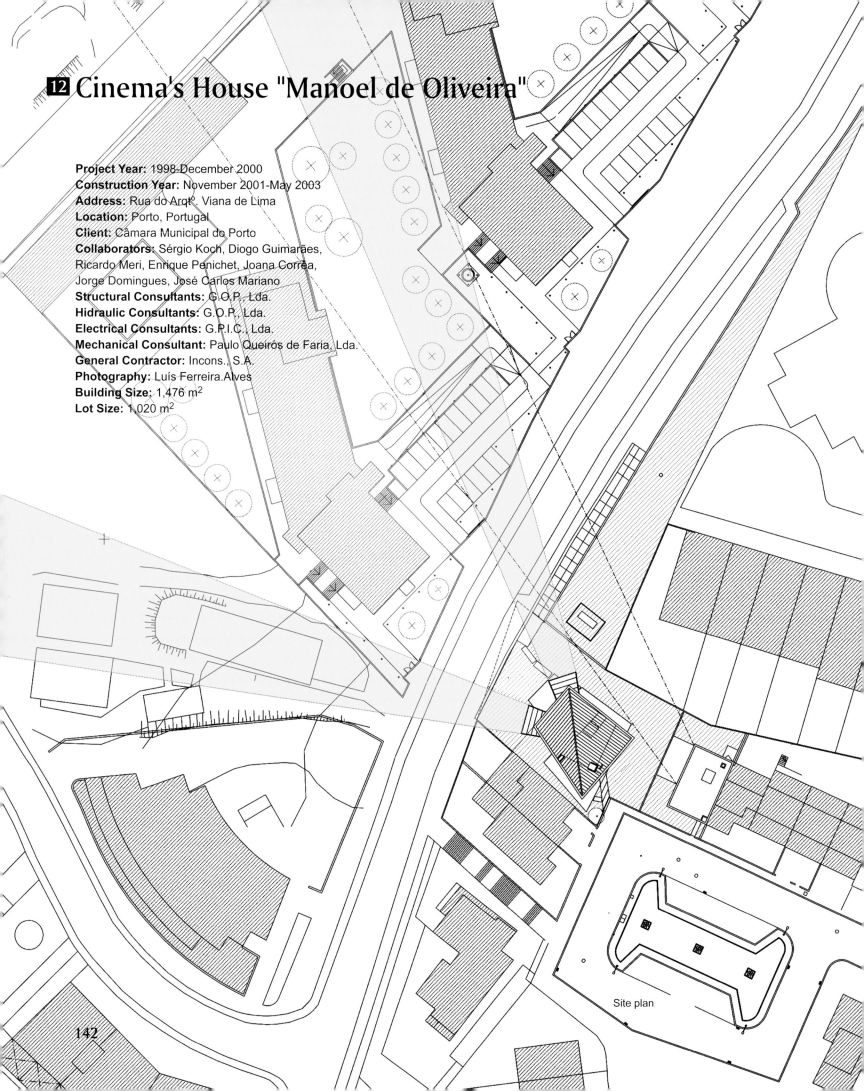

⓬ Cinema's House "Manoel de Oliveira"

Project Year: 1998-December 2000
Construction Year: November 2001-May 2003
Address: Rua do Arqtº. Viana de Lima
Location: Porto, Portugal
Client: Câmara Municipal do Porto
Collaborators: Sérgio Koch, Diogo Guimarães,
Ricardo Meri, Enrique Penichet, Joana Corrêa,
Jorge Domingues, José Carlos Mariano
Structural Consultants: G.O.P., Lda.
Hidraulic Consultants: G.O.P., Lda.
Electrical Consultants: G.P.I.C., Lda.
Mechanical Consultant: Paulo Queirós de Faria, Lda.
General Contractor: Incons., S.A.
Photography: Luís Ferreira.Alves
Building Size: 1,476 m²
Lot Size: 1,020 m²

Site plan

The building presents a cubic form, similar to the surrounding houses, suffering some inflections for best to answer to the dimensions of the lot - inclined roof and trapeze for the auditorium. The fact that two towers, distanced 35 metres, with 15 storeys are foreseen, made us want to split the space of the library in two, focusing them towards the river and the sea. Outwardly, the covering will be in zinc, the floor 1 with a dark grey monopaste and the groundfloor covered with an unpolished inox foil. Inwardly the ceilings will be acoustic, the walls plastered and the pavements of the compartments also in a dark wood, being the hall and the stairways in a softened grey marble. The project also includes an access and external arrangements towards the new street, on the south of the construction. With this tail the building is no longer a "fly" but I want to see which way the "cat" jumps.

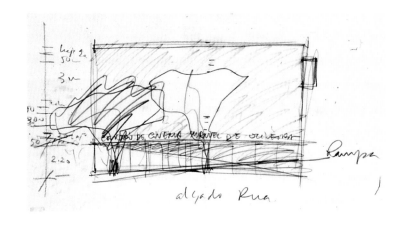

alçado Rua

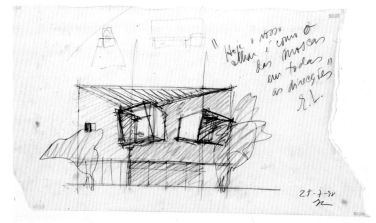

"Hoje o nosso olhar é como ò das moscas em todas as direcções"
R.L.

28-7-98

alçado Nar

25/7/98

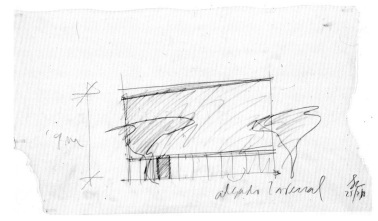

9m

alçado Transeral

25/7/98

144

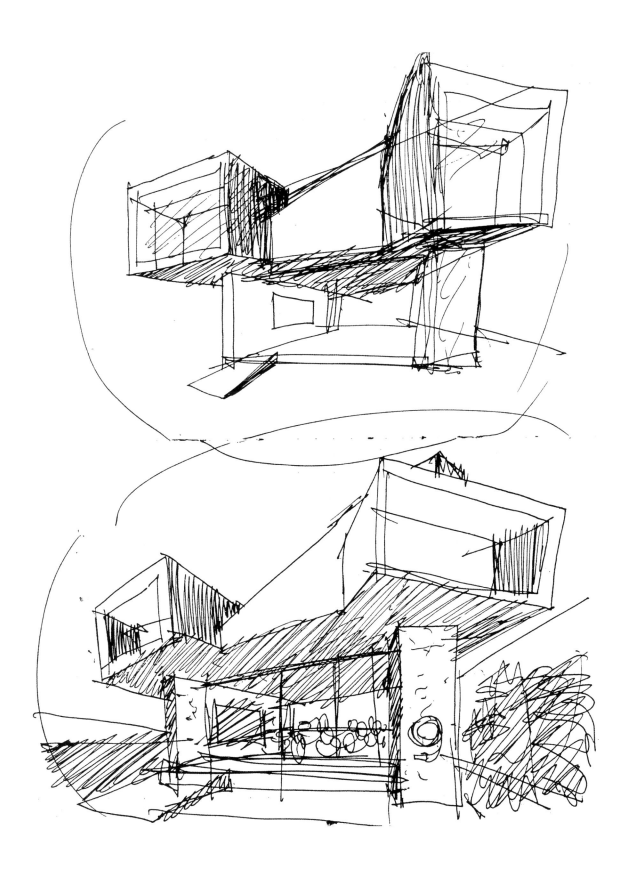

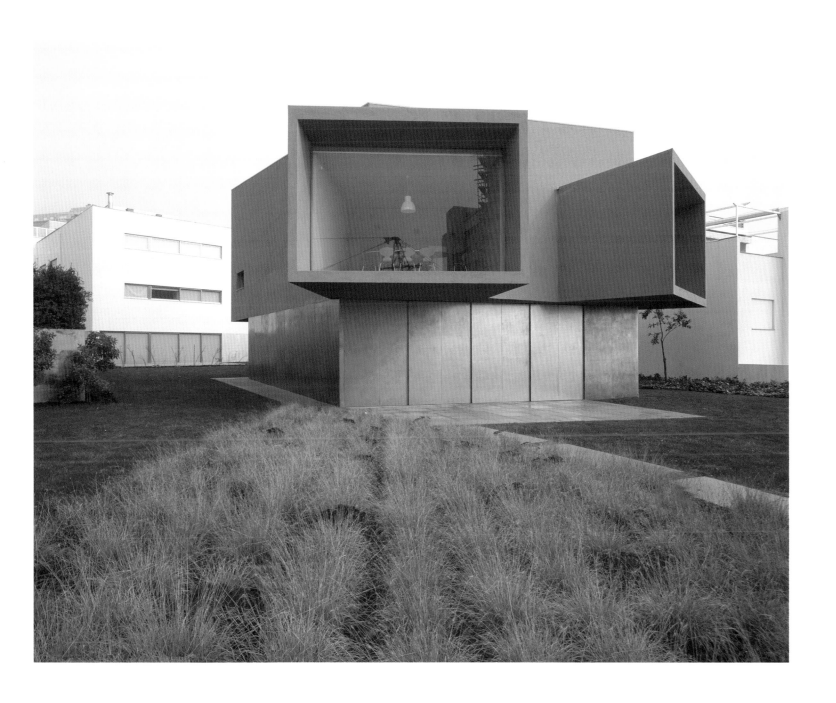

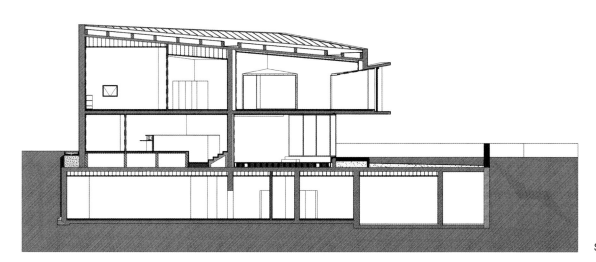

Section 1

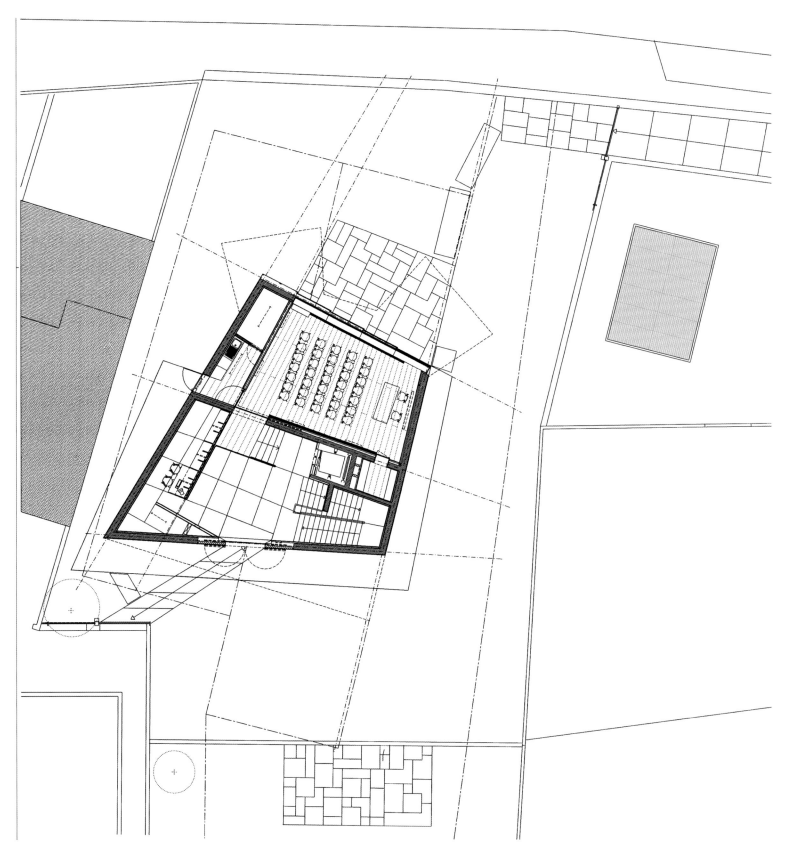

Ground floor plan

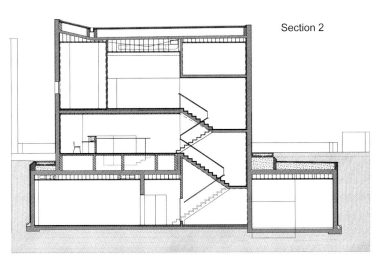

Section 2

149

Basement floor plan

150

Constructive section

1. Pine wood joist
2. Zinc plate
3. Roofmate 4cm
4. Plywood 25mm
5. Ytong brick
6. Zinc plate
7. Roofmate 3cm
8. Vireo coating ref: "visolast"
9. Waterproof regularisation
10. Radkon
11. Concrete
12. False ceiling substructure
13. Rock of high density
14. Wilhelmi Werke acoustic coating
15. Waterproof plasterboard
16. Polystyrene thermal insulation (Wallmate)
17. Air-conditioner grid
18. Supporting box
19. Humus
20. Ytong brick
21. Delta drain
22. Wallmate 4cm
23. Sikaplan PVC screen
24. Geotextile
25. Regularisation screed with 2% drop
26. Lightweight concrete
27. Drip ruff
28. Radkon
29. Wallmate 2cm
30. Waterproof regularisation
31. Vireo coating ref.: "visolast"
32. Coated shutters of stripped and anodised aluminium 5mm
33. Granite 8cm
34. Screed with regularisation
35. Geotextile
36. Roofmate 4cm
37. Sikaplan PVC screen
38. Geotextile
39. Regularisation screed with 2% drop
40. Lightweight concrete
41. Rock of high density
42. Wilhelmi Werke acoustic coating

43. Roller of the "blackout" type blind
44. Technal aluminium frame-double rail "Serial Number GK"
45. Granite block
46. Brick 7cm
47. Regularisation
48. Granite step
49. Brass grid
50. Pine wood floor
51. Waterproof concrete with Radkon
52. Waterproof regularisation
53. Waterproof concrete with Bentofix
54. Wallmate 4cm
55. Delta drain
56. Drain
57. False ceiling substructure
58. Wilhelmi Werke acoustic coating
59. Epoxy
60. Filling

61. Polystyrene thermal insulation
62. Regularisation
63. Zinc vale
64. Granulated cork
65. Roofmate 2cm
66. Ytong brick
67. Plywood 25mm
68. Roofmate 4cm
69. Pine wood joist
70. Rock of high density
71. Waterproof plasterboard
72. Pine wood floor
73. Rock of high density
74. Pine wood joist
75. Regularisation
76. Granulated cork
77. Ytong brick
78. Bedding mortar
79. Pine wood floor
80. Pine wood joist
81. Regularisation

82. Polystyrene thermal insulation
83. Filling/Settlement
84. Marble
85. Rock of high density
86. Waterproof plasterboard
87. Polystyrene thermal insulation
88. Diffusing plague
89. Marble
90. Coating screed
91. Regularisation
92. Floor heating tube
93. Pine wood floor
94. Rock of high density
95. Pine wood joist
96. Regularisation
97. Rock of high density
98. Wilhelmi Werke acoustic coating
99. Marble 3cm
100. Layer of regularisation
101. Layer of filling and concrete paving flags 5cm

102. Ytong brick wall to support the paving flags
103. Vireo coating ref.: "visolast"
104. Waterproof regularisation
105. Radkon
106. Concrete
107. Wallmate
108. Waterproof plasterboard
109. False ceiling substructure
110. Wilhelmi Werke acoustic coating
111. Rock of high density
112. Vireo coating ref.: "visolast"
113. Waterproof regularisation
114. Wallmate 2cm
115. Drip ruff
116. Radkon
117. "Brickslot-simple" drainage system
118. Concrete foundation
119. False ceiling substructure
120. Wilhelmi Werke acoustic coating

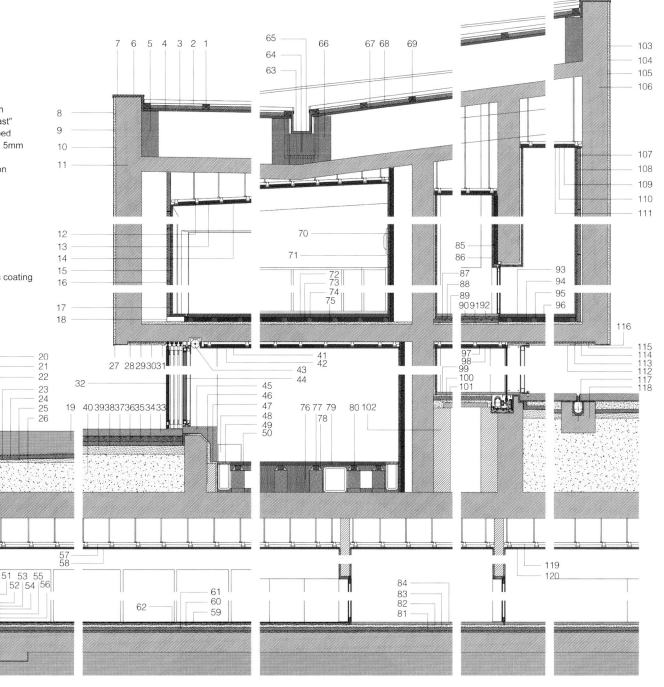

153

13 Braga Municipal Stadium

Project Year: January 2000
Construction Year: January 2002
Address: Monte Crasto, Parque Norte, Braga
Location: Braga, Portugal
Owner: Braga Town Hall
Client: Braga Town Hall
Collaborators: Carlo Nozza, Ricardo Meri, Enrique Penichet, Atsushi Hoshina, Diego Setien, Carmo Correia, Luisa Rosas
Landscape Design: Daniel Monteiro, Braga
Structural Consultants: AFA Associados, Oporto
Electrical Consultants: Rodrigues Gomes & Associados, Oporto
Mechanical Consultants: Rodrigues Gomes & Associados, Oporto
Road Layout Consultants: AFA Associados, Oporto
Planning and Roof Construction Consultants:
Arup Associates, London
Geological Research Consultants: Cêgê, Lisbon
Health and Safety Project Consultants: Gerisco, Lisbon
Roof Cable Structure Planning: Tensoteci, Italy
Wind Tunel Consultants: RWDI Inc., Ontario, Canada
Wind Effect Studies Consultants: DMI, Danmark
General Contractor: SOARES DA COSTA / ASSOC / ACE, Oporto
Photographer: Luís Ferreira Alves
Building Size: 30,000 Seats
Cost: 75,000,000 Euros

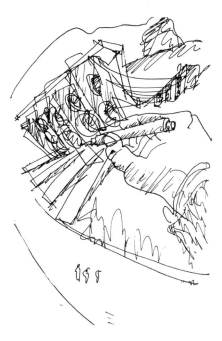

The Braga Municipal Stadium is situated within the Dume Sports Park on the northern slope of Monte Castro. The location was chosen in order to avoid making a dam along the water's edge in the valley. The alternative would have been to move it further to the west up against the hill, like a Roman amphitheatre. Nowadays football is big entertainment, hence the decision to have only two rows of seats. Initially, the roof was to look like a long continuous visor (ref. Siza / Expo), but it was eventually modelled on the Peruvian Inca bridges. With a height of 40 metres, the stadium will be up against two squares with the same sloping. This will enable the stadium building to serve as an anchor point for any future development in the area as the city expands northwards.

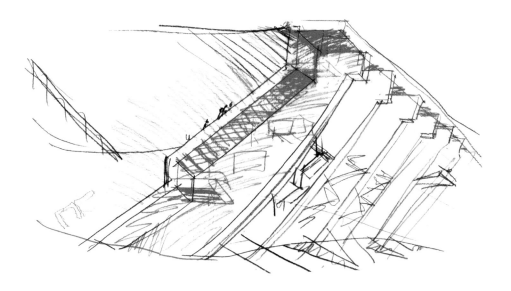

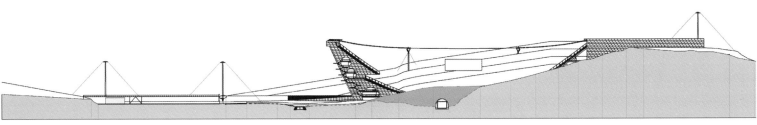

Northwest elevation

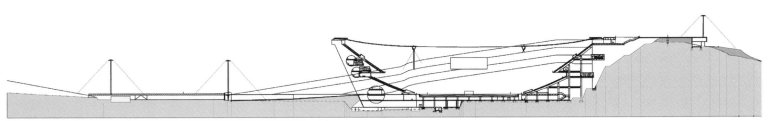

Northwest elevation

157

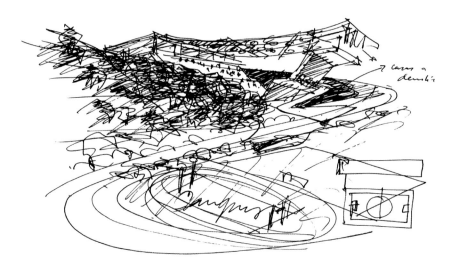

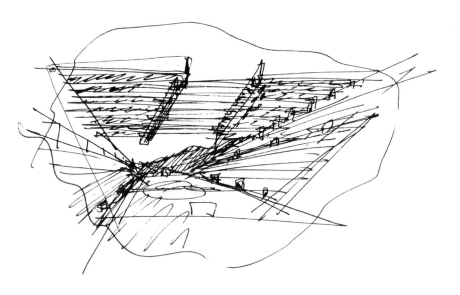

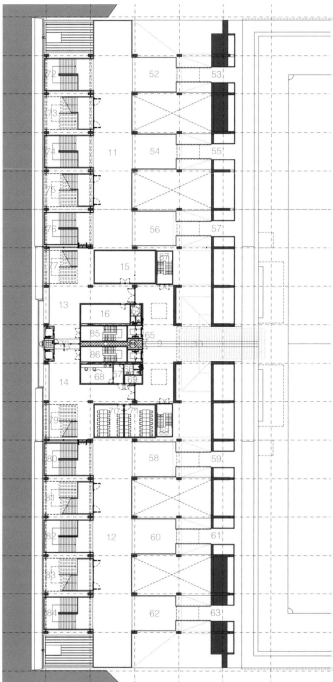

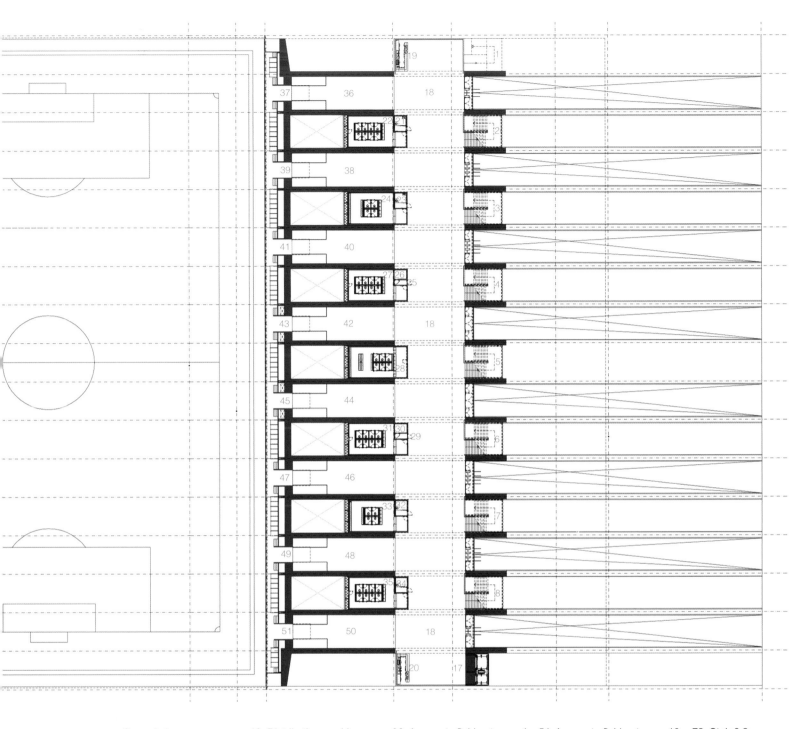

Ground plan	18. Distribution corridor	36. Access to field entrance 1	54. Access to field entrance 10	72. Stair 8.2
1. Ramp	19. Bar 1	37. Field entrance 1	55. Field entrance 10	73. Stair 9.3
2. Stair 1	20. Bar 2	38. Access to field entrance 2	56. Access to field entrance 11	74. Stair 9.4
3. Stair 2	21. Disabled toilet 1	39. Field entrance 2	57. Field entrance 11	75. Stair 10.3
4. Stair 3	22. Toilet 1	40. Access to field entrance 3	58. Access to field entrance 14	76. Stair 10.4
5. Stair 4	23. Disabled toilet 2	41. Field entrance 3	59. Field entrance 14	77. Stair 11.3
6. Stair 5	24. Toilet 2	42. Access to field entrance 4	60. Access to field entrance 15	(VIP's / UEFA)
7. Stair 6	25. Electrical quarter access	43. Field entrance 4	61. Field entrance 15	78. Technical area 2
8. Stair 7	26. Electrical quarter 1	44. Access to field entrance 5	62. Access to entrance field 16	79. Stair 12.3 (press)
9. Players' atrium	27. Toilet 3	45. Field entrance 5	63. Entrance field 16	80. Stair 13.4
10. Field access	28. Toilet 4	46. UEFA meeting room	64. Bathroom 1	81. Stair 13.3
11. Distribution corridor 1	29. Electrical quarter access	47. Field entrance 6	65. Technical area	82. Stair 14.4
12. Distribution corridor 2	30. Electrical quarter 2	48. Access to field entrance 7	66. Bathroom 2	83. Stair 14.3
13. VIP atrium	31. Toilet 5	49. Field entrance 7	67. Hall	84. Stair 15.2
14. Journalist atrium	32. Disabled toilet 3	50. Access to field entrance 8	68. Working facilities	85. Stair 11.4 - VIP
15. UEFA room	33. Toilet 6	51. Field entrance 8	69. Electrical quarter	86. Stair 12.4 - press
16. Grass storage	34. Disabled toilet 4	52. Access to field entrance 9	70. Working facilities	87. Stair 16.1
17. Lift access	35. Toilet 7	53. Field entrance 9	71. Working facilities	88. Stair 17.1

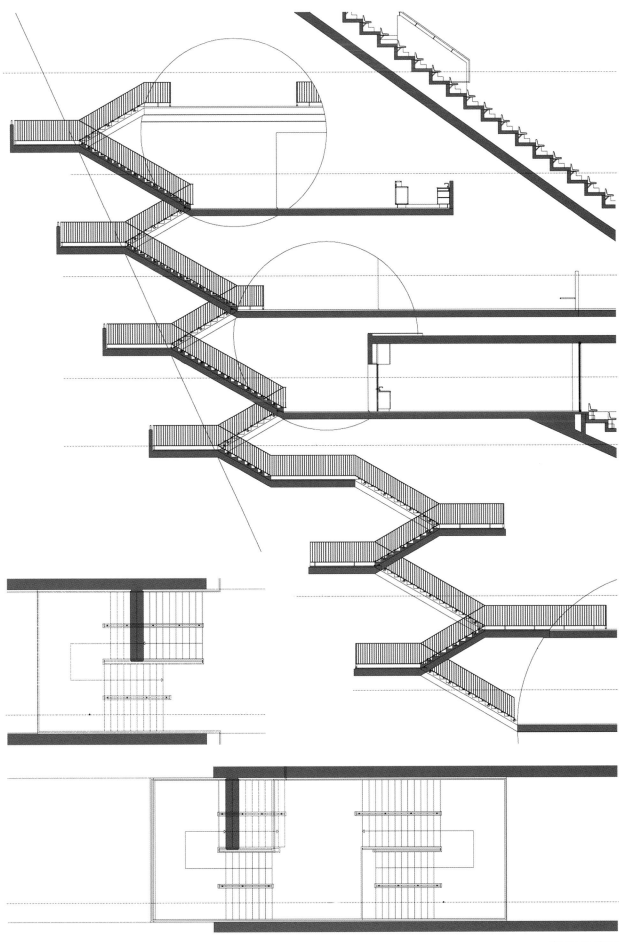

Stairs sections

165

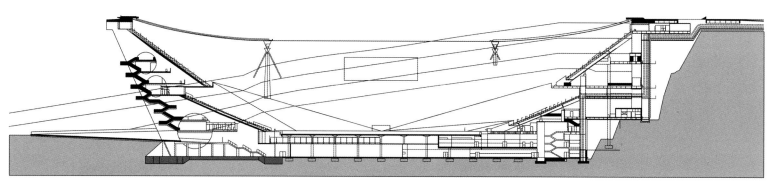

Longitudinal section

166

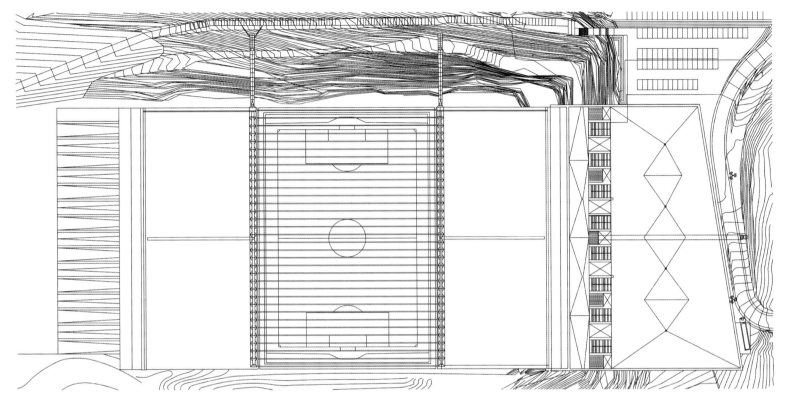

Roof plan

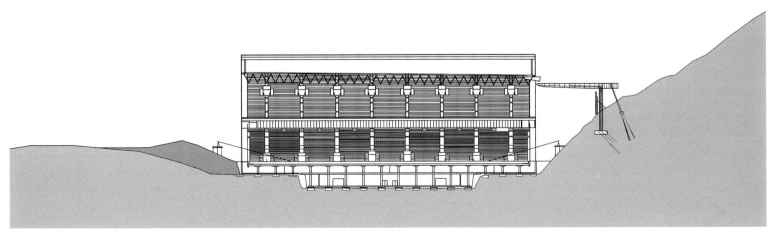

Transverse section

167

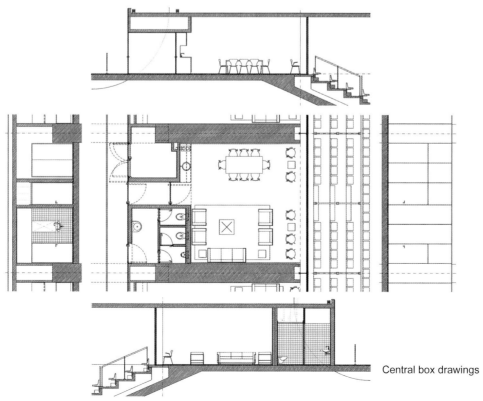

Central box drawings

⒕ 2 Houses in Ponte de Lima

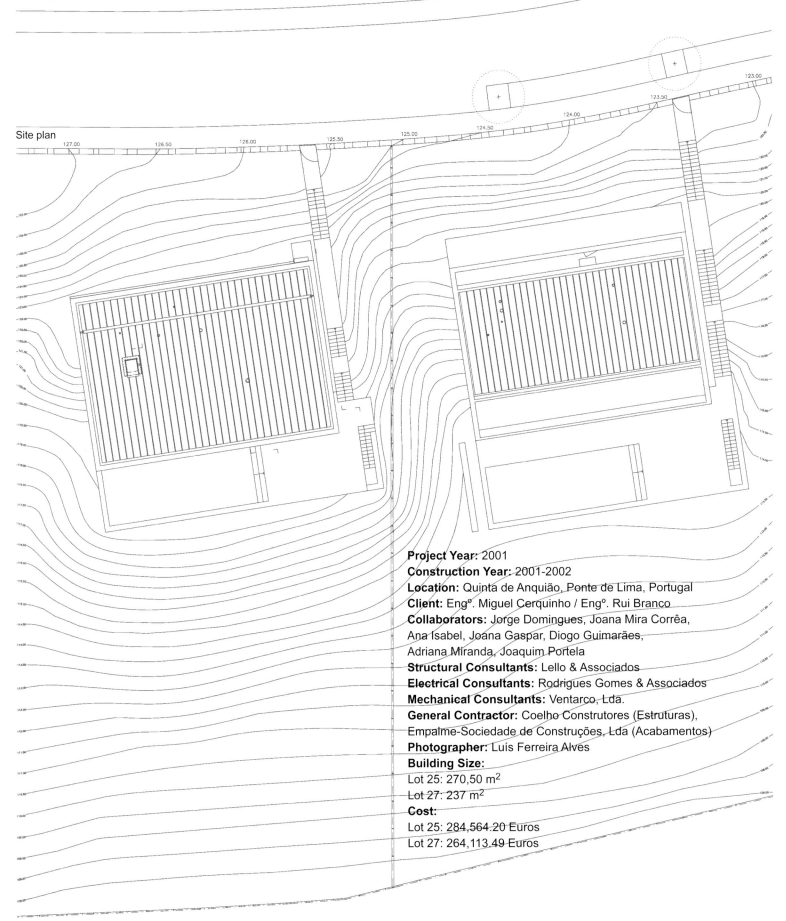

Site plan

Project Year: 2001
Construction Year: 2001-2002
Location: Quinta de Anquião, Ponte de Lima, Portugal
Client: Engº. Miguel Cerquinho / Engº. Rui Branco
Collaborators: Jorge Domingues, Joana Mira Corrêa,
Ana Isabel, Joana Gaspar, Diogo Guimarães,
Adriana Miranda, Joaquim Portela
Structural Consultants: Lello & Associados
Electrical Consultants: Rodrigues Gomes & Associados
Mechanical Consultants: Ventarco, Lda.
General Contractor: Coelho Construtores (Estruturas),
Empalme-Sociedade de Construções, Lda (Acabamentos)
Photographer: Luís Ferreira Alves
Building Size:
Lot 25: 270,50 m²
Lot 27: 237 m²
Cost:
Lot 25: 284,564.20 Euros
Lot 27: 264,113.49 Euros

170

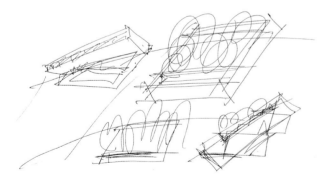

In my architecture, I intended to be thoughtful and fraught with the doubts that assailed design and construction, yet meanwhile rational, acknowledging contradictions and contrasts. The two detached residences with swimming pool at Ponte de Lima are a case in point. They represent two contrasting approaches to building on high-constraint terrain - here a steep slope. This is a very bended site, and the two houses are with the same programme. There are two themes to essay: to be enveloped by the landscape, where the cave from the inside is low-levelling, imminent; to raise the pendent where the look is high, distant, in depth until the mountain. Two houses, one programme, two essays, which have no meaning if separated. As F. Távora used to say in his classes: "…in architecture the opposite is also true."

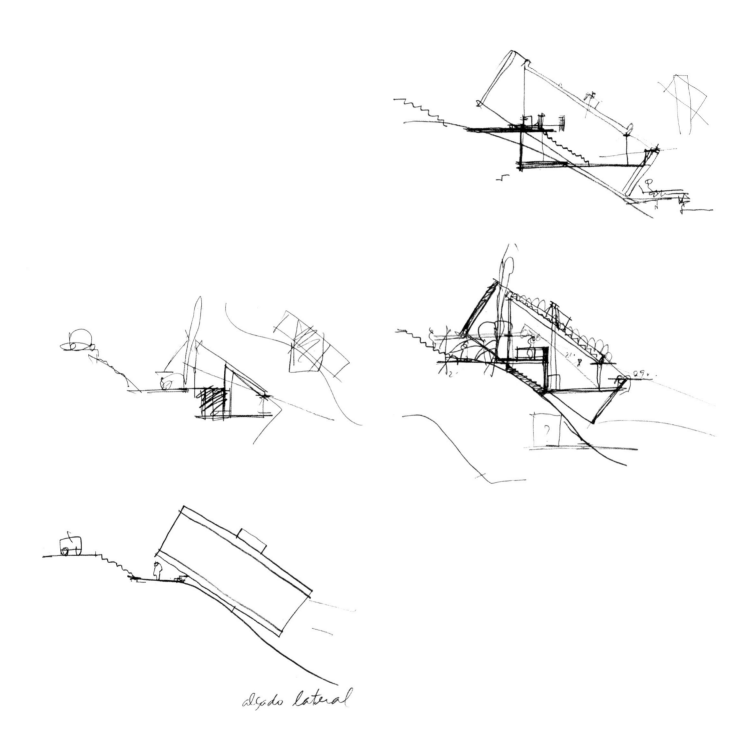

alçado lateral

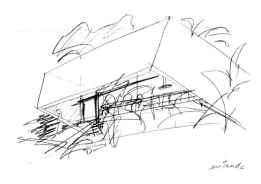

entrada

174

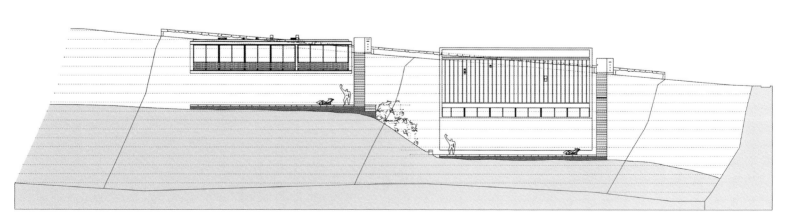

Street elevation

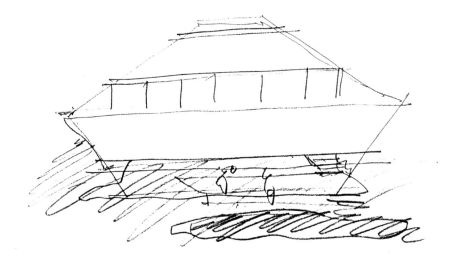

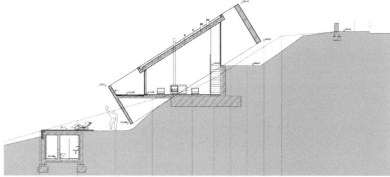

Section 1

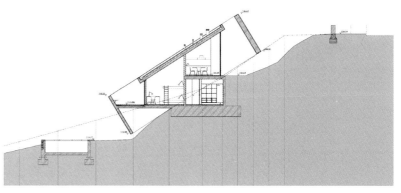

Section 2

177

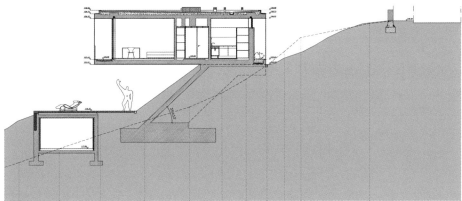

Transverse section

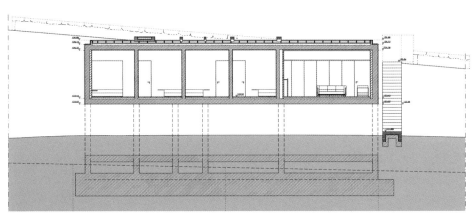

Longitudinal section

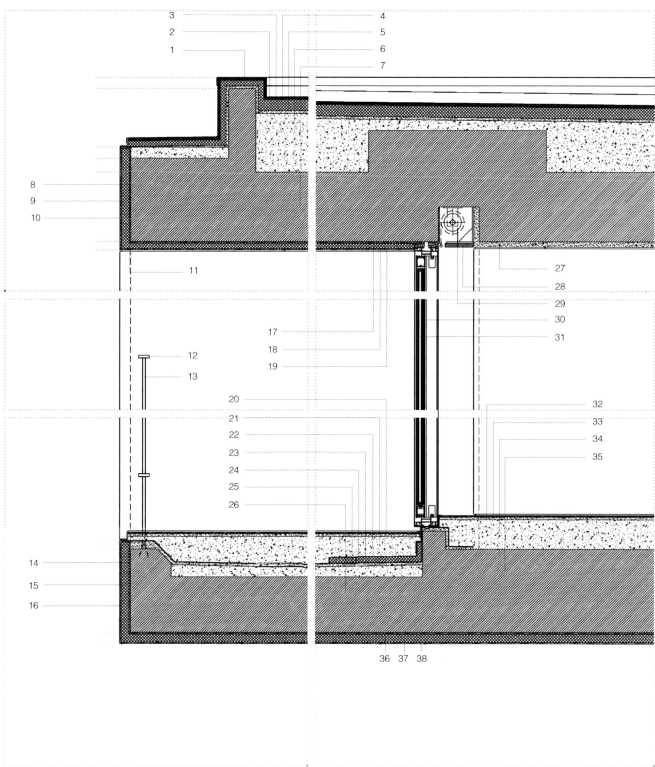

Constructive section (House 1)

1. Zinc ruff
2. Zinc plate (Profile - Camarinha type)
3. "Delta MS Dörken"
4. Roofmate isolation material 4cm
5. Regularisation 1cm
6. Lightweight concrete
7. Slab 20cm
8. Waterproof mortar
9. Expanded polystyrene 3cm
10. Armed coloured concrete 0.5cm
11. Drip pan (5mm vane)
12. Stainless steel flat bar 40x10mm
13. Stainless steel rod φ 10mm

14. Waterproof mortar
15. Expanded polystyrene 3cm
16. Armed and coloured concrete 0.5cm
17. Waterproof mortar
18. Expanded polystyrene 3cm
19. Armed and coloured concrete 0.5cm
20. "Sika" type self-levelling
21. Bedding mortar
22. Armed screed
23. Roofmate isolation material 2cm
24. Asphalt screen
25. Form layer with regularisation
26. Concrete slab 20cm

27. Plaster stucco 2cm
28. Plywood to be painted 15mm
29. Roller blinds - (Type sunscreen)
30. Technal aluminium frame-double rail "Serial Number GK"
31. Double glass of security (6+8+10.2)
32. Sika type self-levelling
33. Regularisation
34. Armed screed 8cm
35. Concrete slab 30cm
36. Waterproof mortar
37. Expanded polystyrene 3cm
38. Armed and coloured concrete 0.5cm

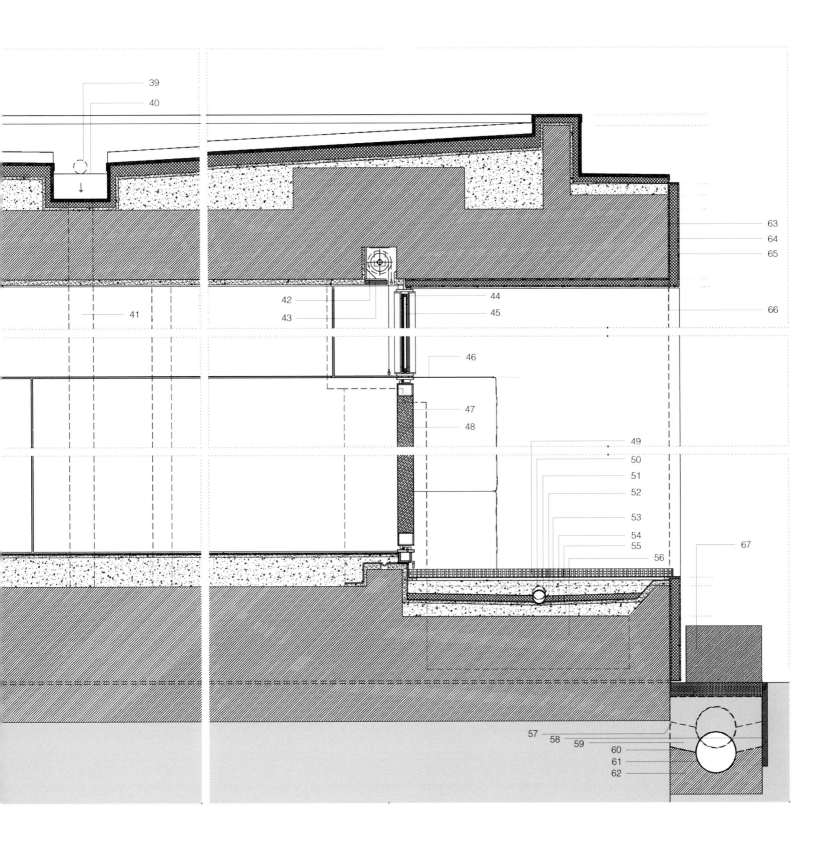

39. "Troplein" 5cm
40. Vale
41. Falling tube 9cm (Air box)
42. Roller blinds - (Type sunscreen)
43. Plywood to be painted 15mm
44. Stainless steel frame
45. Double glass (4+6+8)
46. Granite stone 20cm
47. Stainless steel plate 2mm
48. High density rock

49. Steel grid
50. Porous concrete
51. Drain
52. Geotextile
53. Roofmate isolation material 2cm
54. Asphalt screen
55. Form layer with regularisation
56. Concrete slab 20cm
57. Sarrisca 5cm
58. Ruler pine 2cm

59. Layer of gravel 20cm
60. Geotextile
61. Geodrain tube, diameter 150mm
62. Concrete screed
63. Waterproof mortar
64. Expanded polystyrene 3cm
65. Armed and coloured concrete 0.5cm
66. Drip pan (5mm vane)
67. Granite step

181

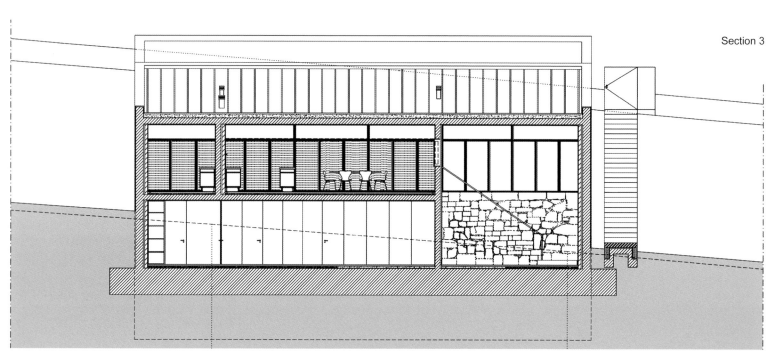

Section 3

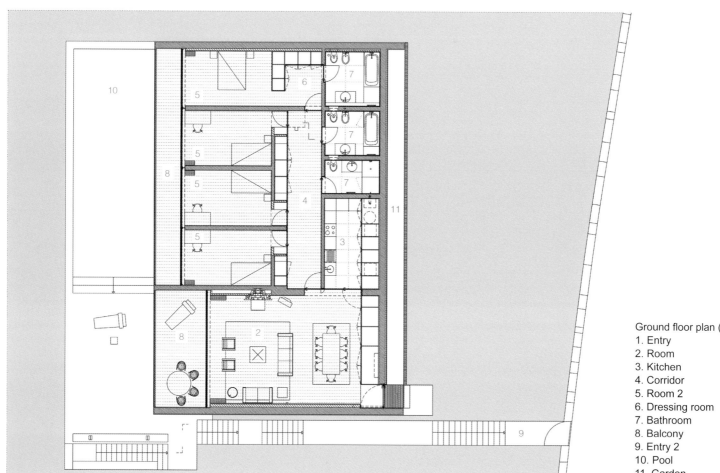

Ground floor plan (House 1)
1. Entry
2. Room
3. Kitchen
4. Corridor
5. Room 2
6. Dressing room
7. Bathroom
8. Balcony
9. Entry 2
10. Pool
11. Garden

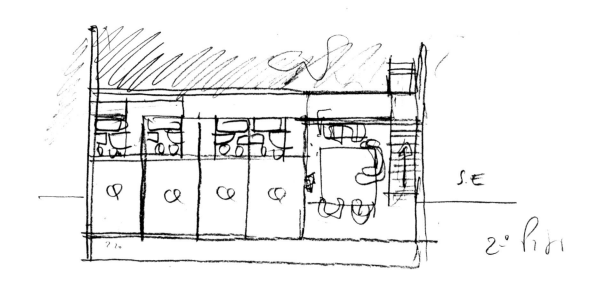

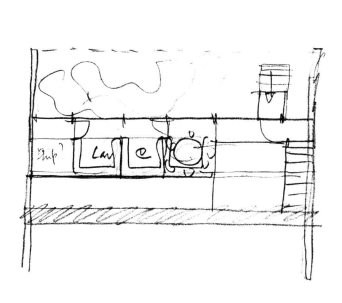

15 Contemporary Art Museum in Braganca

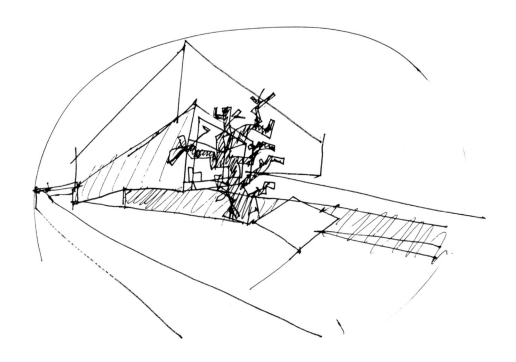

Project Year: 2002
Construction Year: March 2008
Address: Rua Abílio Beça, 105
Locality: Bragança, Portugal
Client: Bragança City Hall
Collaborators: Joaquim Portela, Teresa Fonseca,
Tiago Coelho, Jorge Domingues, Maria Vasconcelos,
Diogo Machado Lima, Ana Fortuna, Cândida Corrêa de Sá,
Patrícia Diogo, Cátia Bernardo, Ricardo Prata, Susana Monteiro
Structural Consultants: AFA
Electrical Consultants: AFA
Mechanical Consultants: AFA
General Contractor: FDO
Photographer: Luís Ferreira Alves

The Braganca Contemporary Art Museum consists of several parts. First, construction of a new building, with a temporary exhibitions area, 240 square metres and 8.30 metres high, is capable of receiving any exhibition that submits to the conditionings of the international legislation (light, ventilation, air conditioned, setting services, etc). Second, rehabilitation of the building, Solar Veiga Cabral, former "Banco de Portugal", that will receive the permanent exhibition on the first floor. The ground floor will function as a library, reception and restaurant, as well as other adjacent services. Third, the two buildings will be connected by a new volume, which corresponds to the proposed programme: circulation between temporary and permanent exhibitions; complementary programme to the museological activity, such as: educative service, administrative cabinet, and museology technical cabinet. After this three volumes' restructuration, there are left some interstitial spaces, which will be fulfilled these ways: trucks' access ramp, for exhibitions loading and unloading, small yard to park cars, pedestrian ramp, from Emídio Navarro Street to the restaurant's esplanade, which will serve those out of the regular working hours. And, this operation obliges to the use of the pre-defined materials, in Emídio Navarro Street project, because without this, the museum wouldn't be integrated in an urban requalification operation, but would be one more insolite object.

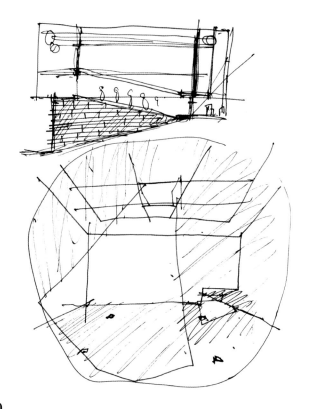

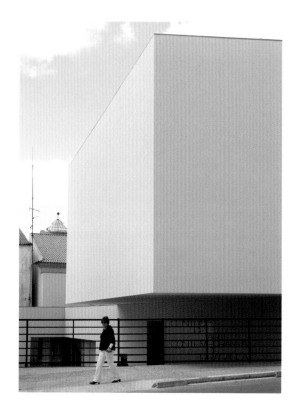

190

Section 1

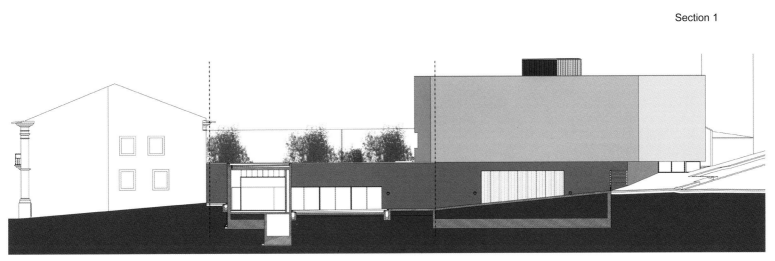

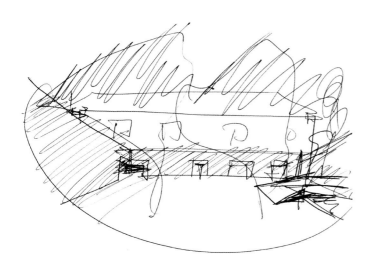

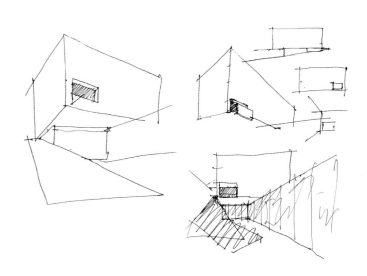

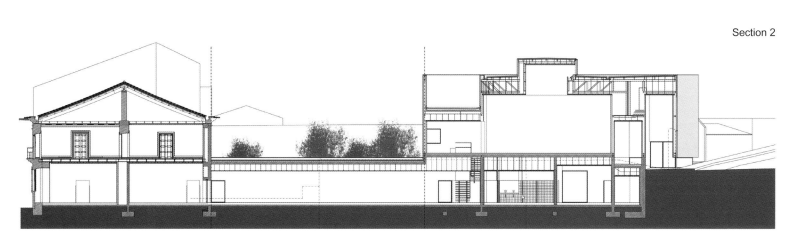

193

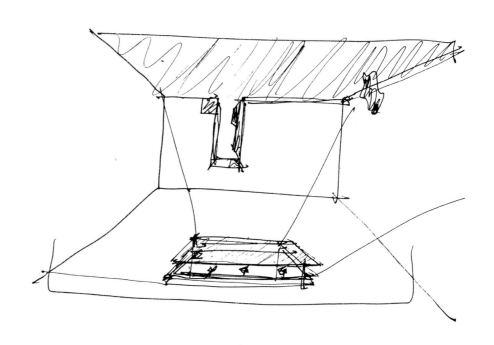

194

Longitudinal section of temporary exhibition room
1. Galvanised steel structure in plasterboard system
2. Double rock 30mm
3. Fireproof plasterboard panel 20mm
4. "Baswaphon" type rigid mineral wool panel 45mm
5. Two layers of "Baswaphon" type acoustic plaster
6. Square tubular steel structure 50x50x3mm
7. Galvanised steel structure in plasterboard system
8. 2x30mm rock
9. Fireproof plasterboard panel 20mm
10. Steel bracket 30x30x3mm
11. "iGuzzinni" type standard illumination gutter 32x32mm
12. Square tubular steel structure 50x50x3mm
13. Bended steel plate 6mm
14. "ERCO-wallwasher" type luminaria, ref.65040
15. "iGuzzini" type standard illumination gutter type 32x32mm
16. Galvanised steel structure in plasterboard system
17. 2x30mm rock
18. Fireproof plasterboard panel 20mm
19. "Baswaphon" type rigid mineral wool panel 45mm
20. Two layers of "Baswaphom" type acoustic plaster
21. 2 x 50 mm rock
22. "Viroc" type cement panel 12mm
23. Fireproof plasterboard panel 20mm
24. "Sika" type self-levelling painted
25. Regularisation 15mm
26. Filling

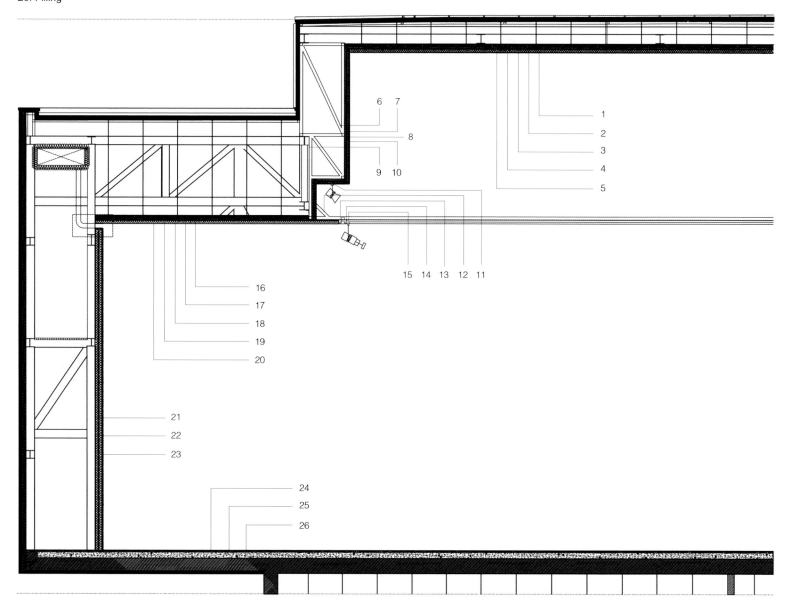

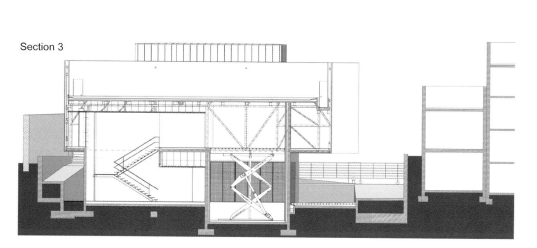

Section 3

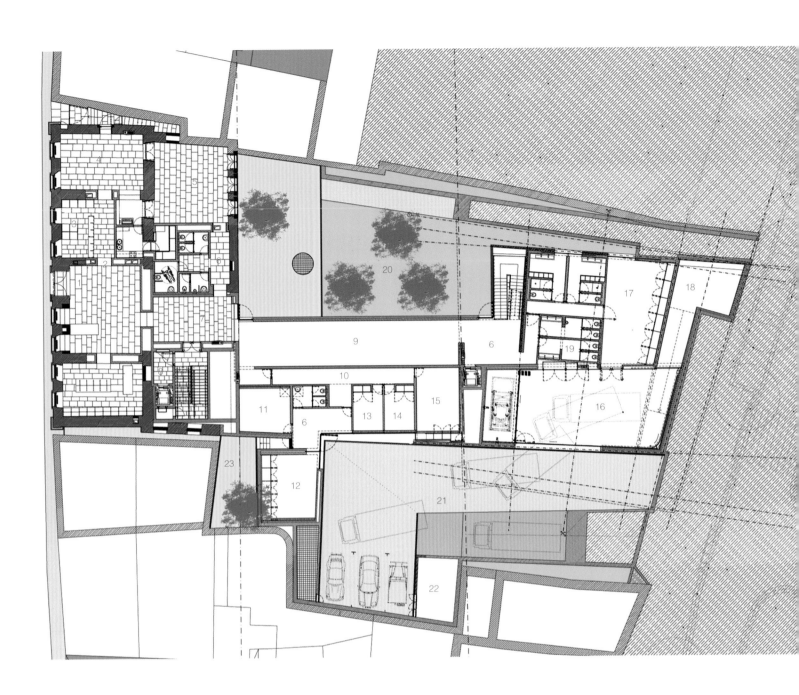

Ground floor plan
1. Entrance
2. Reception
3. Cloakroom
4. Bar
5. Café
6. Hall
7. Temporary exhibitions
   / hall of distribution
8. Elevator
9. Corridor / exhibition
10. Corridor / hall
11. Education service room 1

12. Education service room 2
13. Technical cabinet of museology
14. Cabinet of director
15. Meeting room
16. Reception of works
17. Office
18. Reserved collection
19. Bathroom
20. Public patio
21. Discharge patio
22. Post processing
23. Education service patio

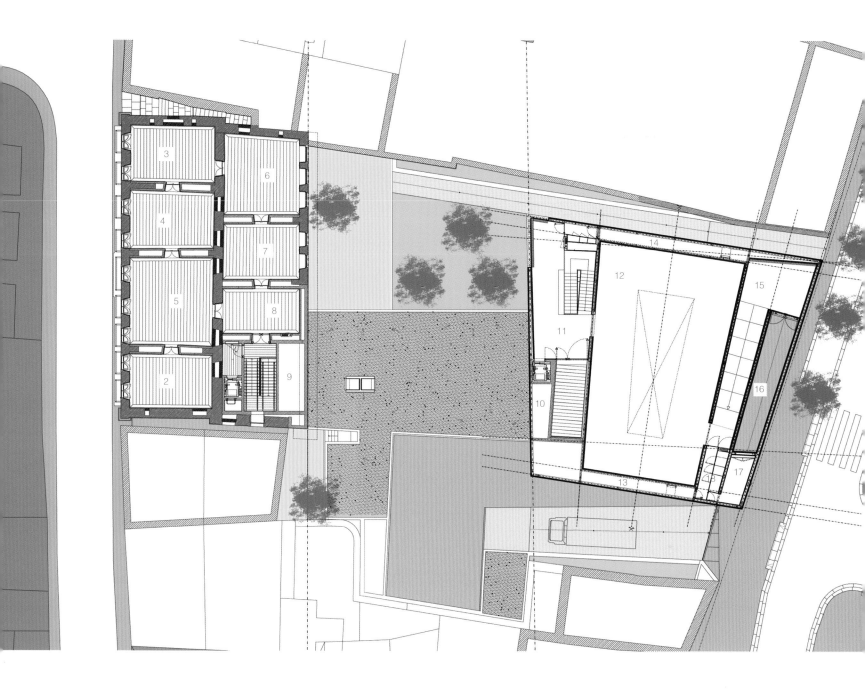

First floor plan
1. Elevator
2. Multipurpose room
3. Permanent exhibition room 1
4. Permanent exhibition room 2
5. Permanent exhibition room 3
6. Permanent exhibition room 4
7. Permanent exhibition room 5
8. Hall of distribution
9. Bandstand 1
10. Bandstand 2
11. Hall/living space
12. Temporary exhibition room
13. Technical area 1
14. Technical area 2
15. Public reception
16. Ramp
17. Security control monitor
18. Access to the technical area

202

16 Row Houses "Quinta da Avenida"

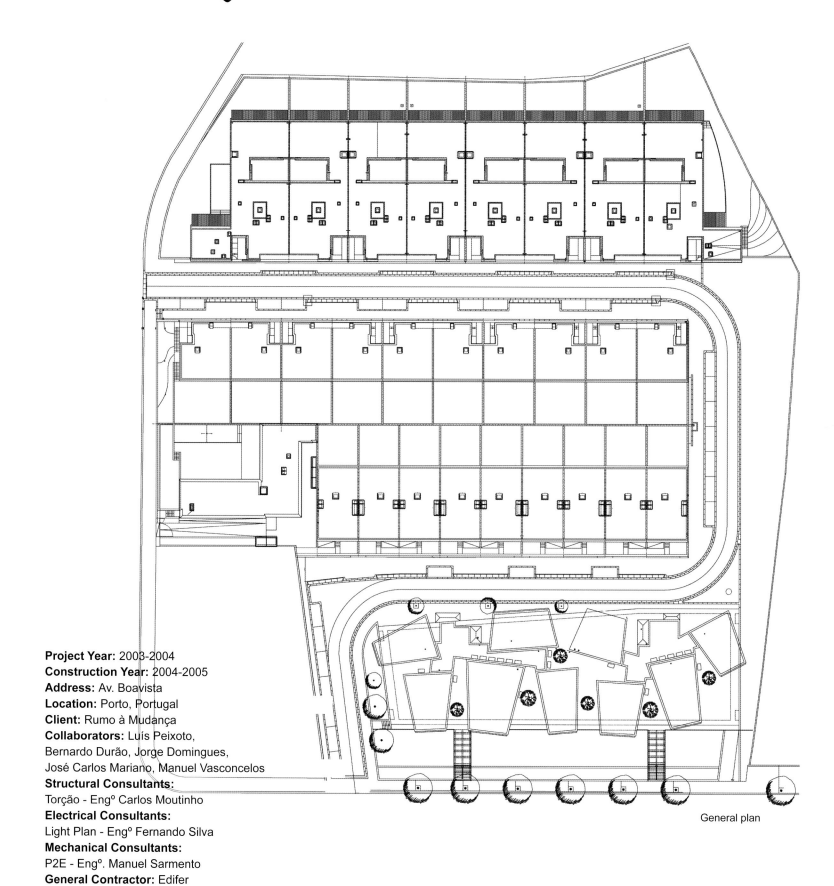

Project Year: 2003-2004
Construction Year: 2004-2005
Address: Av. Boavista
Location: Porto, Portugal
Client: Rumo à Mudança
Collaborators: Luís Peixoto,
Bernardo Durão, Jorge Domingues,
José Carlos Mariano, Manuel Vasconcelos
Structural Consultants:
Torção - Engº Carlos Moutinho
Electrical Consultants:
Light Plan - Engº Fernando Silva
Mechanical Consultants:
P2E - Engº. Manuel Sarmento
General Contractor: Edifer
Photographer: Luís Ferreira Alves

General plan

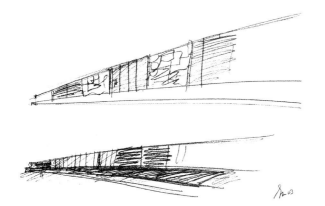

On the basis of a previously approved subdivision on a steep slope, the architects build three row housing typologies set on three platforms. The patio-houses in the upper part, at street level, have a single storey that opens on to the garden. The entrance is generated from a patio/garden on the south side. The three-storey houses are set at the lower level with the transition in between. The entrance and garage are set in the terrace/garden, like in Los Angeles. With the exception of the patio-houses, all the dwellings enjoy views of the park.

206

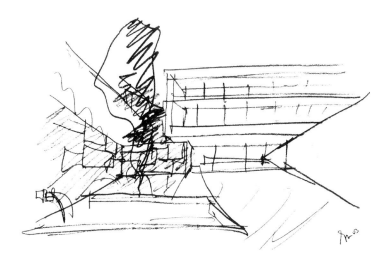

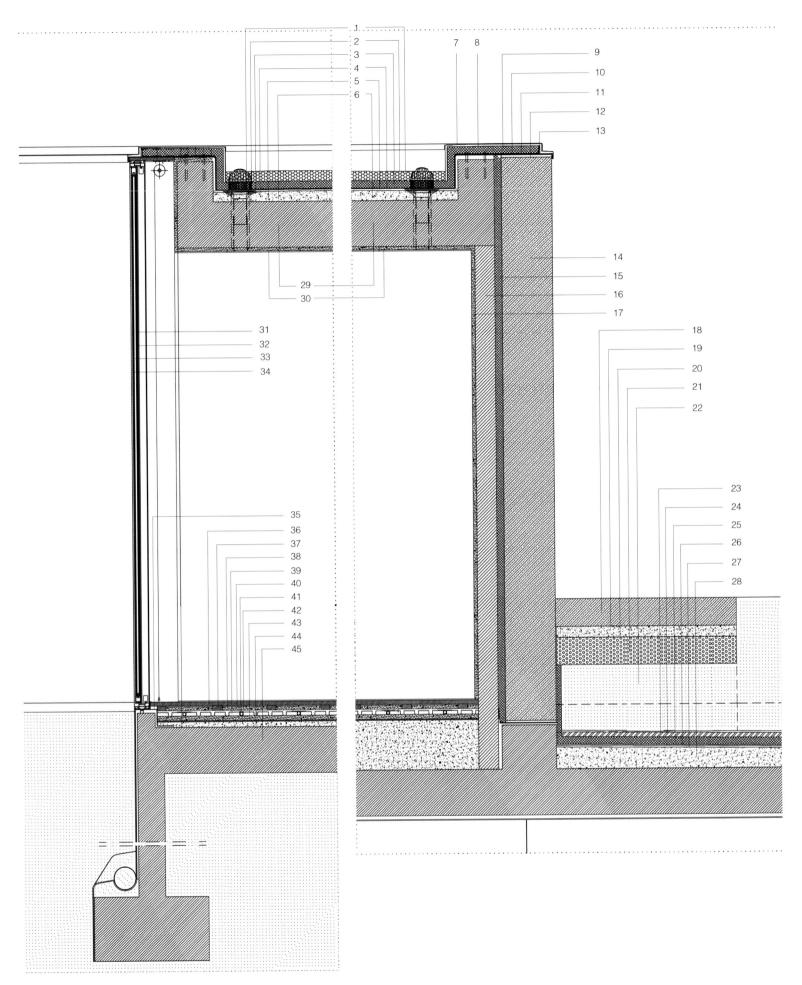

Constructive section (Facing)
1. Cobble coverage
2. Geotextile screen
3. Roofmate isolation material 4cm
4. Waterproof canvas
5. Regularisation 1cm
6. Form layer
7. No.14 zinc sheet ruff
8. Delta MS Droken screen
9. Roofmate isolation material 4cm
10. Waterproof canvas
11. Steel plate 3mm

12. Regularisation
13. Steel plate 5mm
14. Stone wall 28cm
15. Roofmate isolation material 4cm
16. Brick wall 11
17. "Seral" type synthetic stucco
18. Granite paved 12cm
19. Sand cushion
20. Geotextile
21. Gravel foundation 15cm
22. Humus
23. "Impersep 250" (Imperalum) type screen

24. "Isola platon de 25" (Imperalum)
    type screen
25. Roofmate isolation material 4cm
26. Asphalt screen
27. Regularisation
28. Form layer of lightweight concrete
29. Concrete slab 25cm
30. "Seral" type synthetic stucco
31. Aluminium frames Series GK
    (for details see frames)
32. Laminated glass 8mm (4+4)
33. Air box 10mm

34. Tempered glass 6mm
35. Asphalt screen
36. Afzelia floor 22mm
37. Slat
38. Concrete layer with additive
39. Insulation panel
40. Filling
41. PEX tube
42. Clip for insulation panel
43. PE film
44. LECA
45. Concrete slab 25cm

Ground floor plan (Lot 19)
1. Garage
2. Hall 1
3. Tidy room / hall
4. Tidy room
5. Bathroom 1
6. Tidy room / cellaret
7. Tidy room / office
8. Hall 2
9. Laundry
10. Bathroom 1
11. Maid room

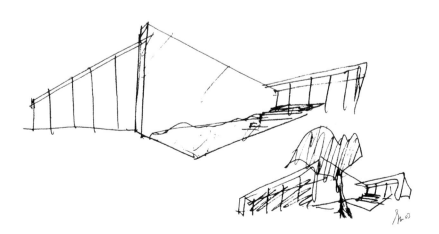

211

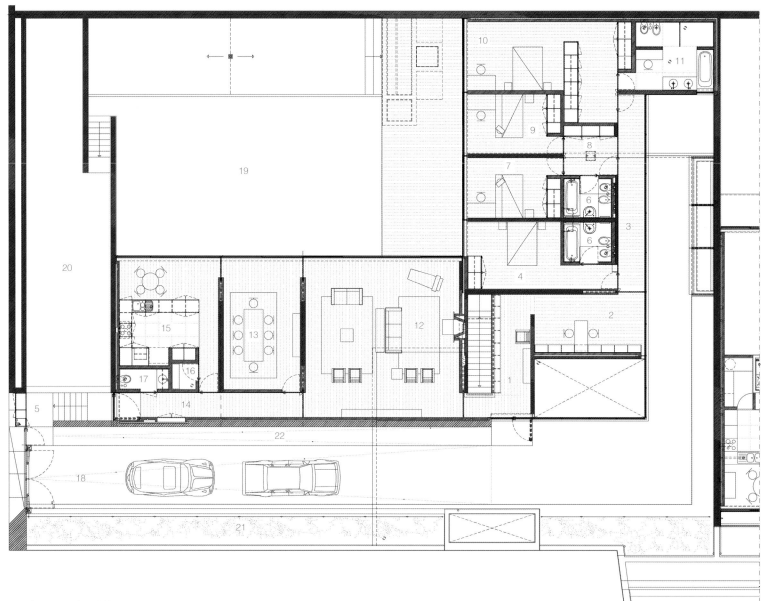

First floor plan (Lot 19)

1. Hall 3
2. Hall 4
3. Hall rooms 1
4. Room 1
5. Bathroom 4
6. Bathroom 5
7. Room 2
8. Hall rooms 2
9. Room 3
10. Bedroom suite
11. Bathroom 6
12. Living room
13. Dining room
14. Hall 5
15. Kitchen
16. Pantry
17. Bathroom 3
18. Garage lighting
19. Patio/garden
20. Garden
21. Plat
22. Route entry

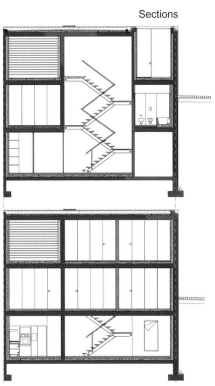

213

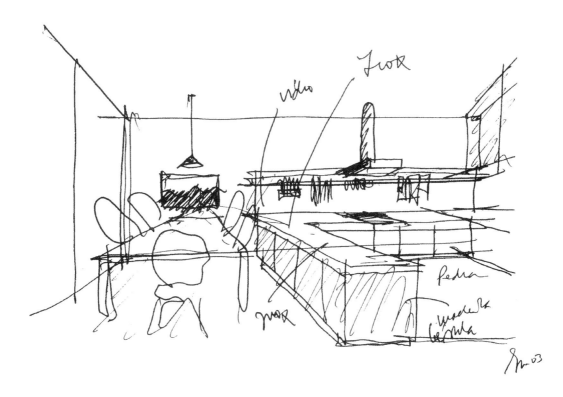

Plan (Lot 1)

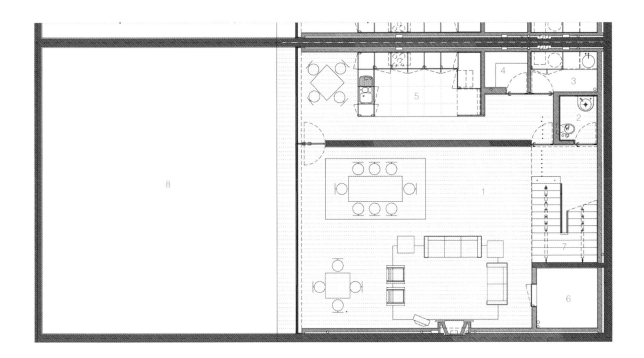

Basement 2 floor plan
(Type B Lot 18)
1. Living / dining room
2. Bathroom 4
3. Laundry
4. Pantry
5. Kitchen
6. Tidy room
7. Stairs
8. Patio / garden

17 House in Maia III

Project Year: 2003-2007
Construction Year: 2007-2010
Address: Rua de Nicolau Nasoni, n.º155
Location: Maia, Portugal
Client: Eng. Tiago Silva
Collaborators: Susana Meirinhos, Joaquim Portela,
Luis Peixoto, Joana Quintanilha, Tiago Santos,
Joana Simões, Junko, Nuno Cordeiro
Structural Consultants: AFAconsult - Eng. Rui Furtado
Electrical Consultants: AFAconsult - Eng. Raul Serafim
Mechanical Consultants: AFAconsult - Eng. João Sousa
Hidraulics Consultants: AFAconsult - Eng. Marta Peleteiro
Gas Consultants: AFAconsult - Eng. Marta Peleteiro
Acustics Consultants: AFAconsult - Eng. Joana Neves da Silva
Security Consultants: AFAconsult - Eng. Maria da Luz Santiago
Exteriors Consultants: Eng. Manuel Pedro Melo
Structural System: Concrete
Major Materials: Concrete, glass and granite
General Contractor: Matrizlda
Photographer: Luis Ferreira Alves
Site Area: 1,071 m²
Built Area: 192 m²
Total Floor Area: 384 m²

Site plan

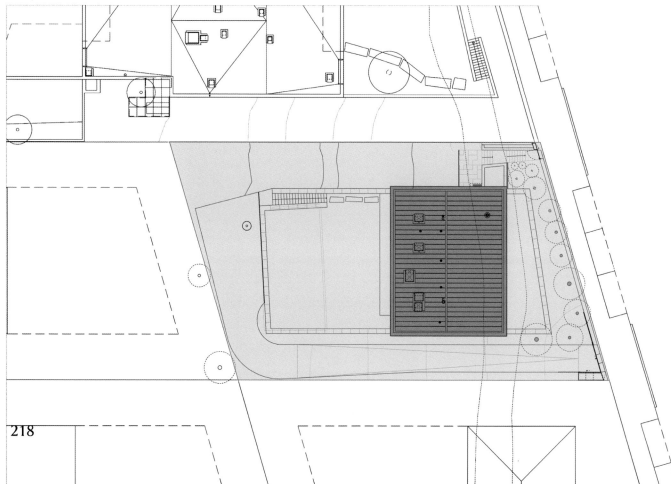

In a land with a strong drop we built two platforms where two volumes are implanted. In the higher volume, in concrete, are the rooms facing east. In the lower volume, of granite, where the other is based, facing west are the rooms and the kitchen, and facing the garden a courtyard that is the garage roof. Along the lot - in the north side - another house that I have made, with the same accuracy by the same company. There are moments like these, that we still believe that we can build well. It´s only a matter of taste and dedication.

Porto, 8th June, 2009, Eduardo Souto de Moura

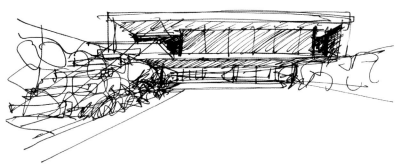

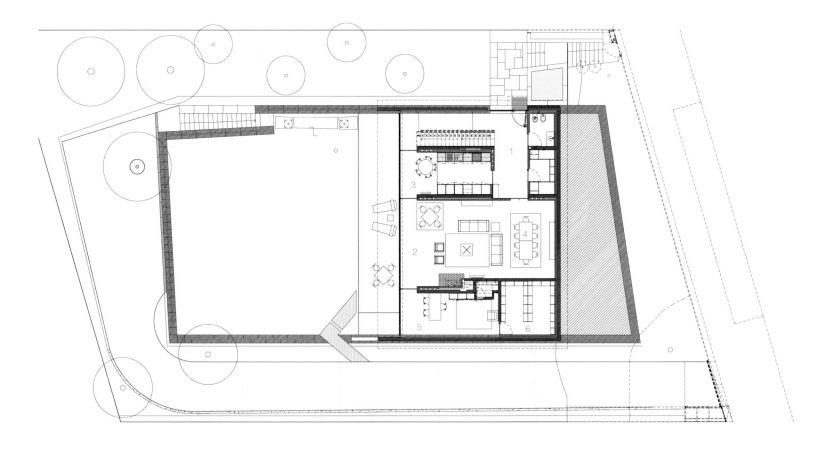

Ground floor plan (Above)
1. Hall
2. Living room
3. Kitchen
4. Dining room
5. Office
6. Library

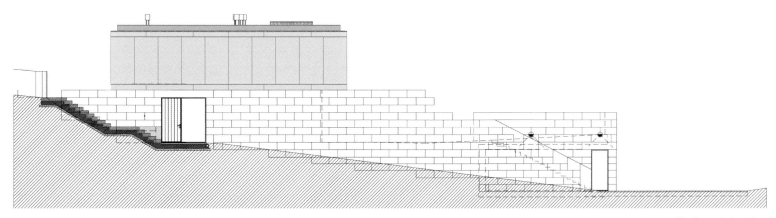

Northwest elevation

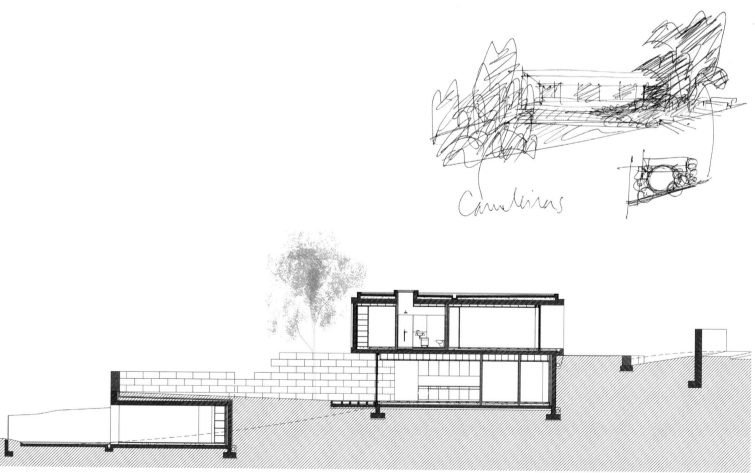

Section 1

223

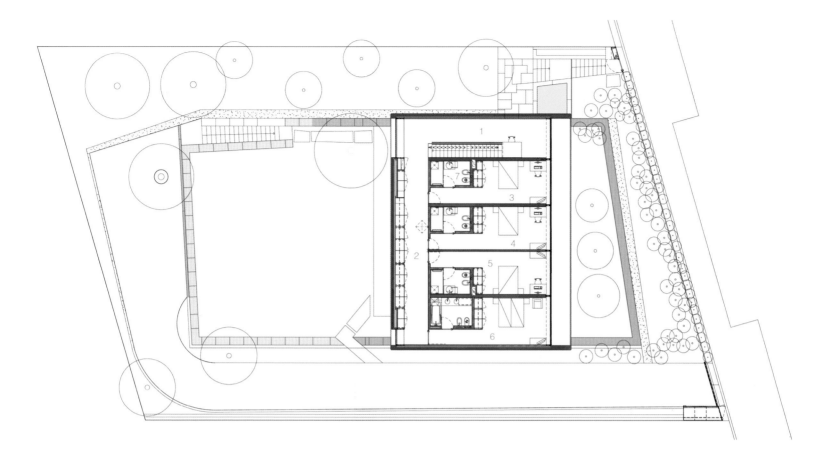

First floor plan (Above)
1. Hall / office
2. Corridor
3. Bedroom 1
4. Bedroom 2
5. Bedroom 3
6. Bedroom 4
7. Bathroom

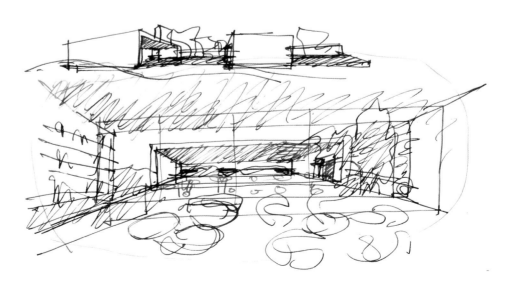

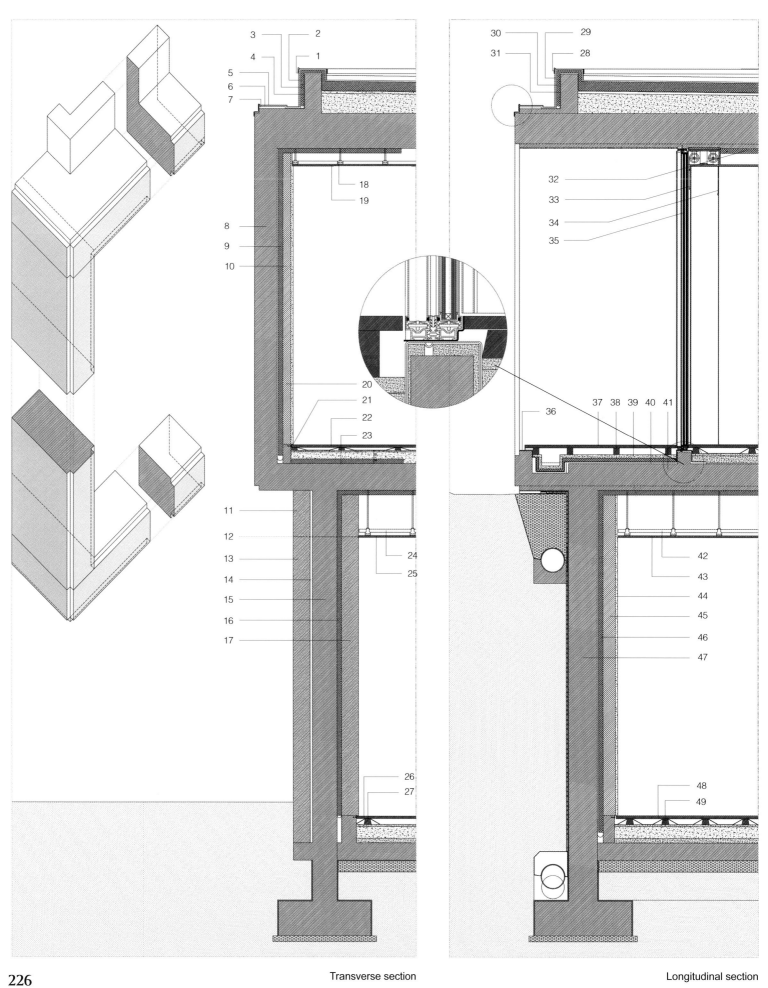

Transverse section

Longitudinal section

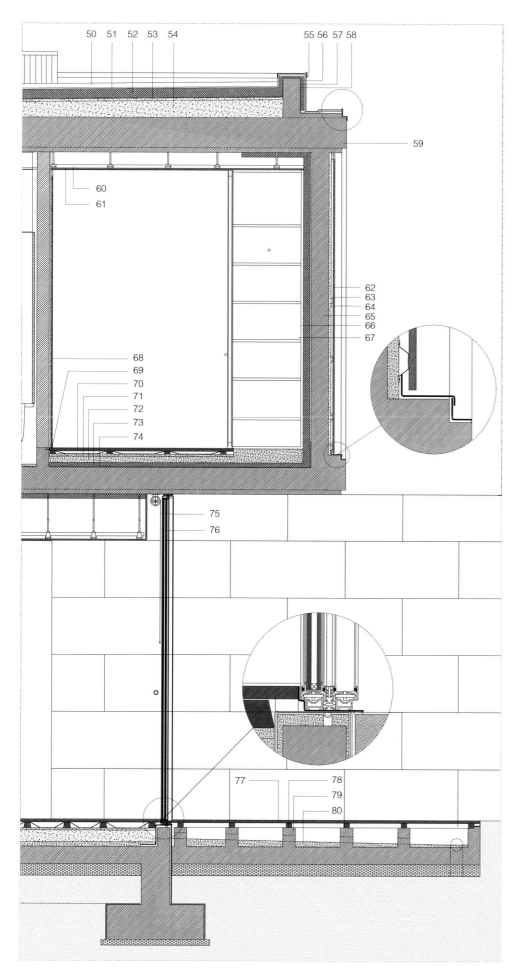

Transverse section
1. No.14 zinc sheet ruff
2. "Delta MS Dörken" screen
3. Roofmate isolation material 3cm
4. Asphalt screen
5. No.14 zinc sheet ruff
6. "Delta MS Dörken" screen
7. Asphalt screen
8. Exposed concrete wall
9. Thermal insulation with Wallmate 4cm
10. Exposed concrete wall
11. Stone masonry
12. Lintel of entry
13. Builders of stone
14. Air box 2cm
15. Concrete wall
16. Thermal insulation with Wallmate 4cm
17. Builders of stone
18. Ceiling suspension system
19. False ceiling of plasterboard
20. "Seral" type synthetic stucco
21. Steel bracket
22. Afzelia floor
23. Slat
24. "Knauf system 112d" type ceiling suspension system
25. False ceiling of plasterboard
26. Afzelia and new RIGA floor
27. Slat
28. No.14 zinc sheet ruff
29. "Delta MS Dörken" screen
30. Roofmate isolation material 3cm
31. Asphalt screen
32. Thermal insulation with Wallmate 4cm
33. "Blackout" type blind
34. "Sun-screen" type blind
35. "Vitrocsa" aluminium frame-double rail
36. Stainless steel bracket
37. Afzelia and new RIGA floor
38. Slat
39. Armed screed
40. Thermal insulation
41. Plastic screen
42. "Knauf system 112d" type ceiling suspension system
43. False ceiling of plasterboard
44. "Seral" type waterproof synthetic stucco
45. Brick wall 11
46. Thermal insulation with Wallmate 4cm
47. Concrete wall
48. Afzelia and new RIGA floor
49. Slat
50. Ruff coverage of No.14 Camarihna type zinc sheet
51. "Delta MS Dörken" screen
52. Roofmate isolation material 8cm
53. Regularisation
54. Form layer of lightweight concrete
55. No.14 zinc sheet ruff
56. "Delta MS Dörken" screen
57. Roofmate isolation material 3cm
58. Asphalt screen
59. Finished exposed concrete with formwork according to the elevation stereotomy
60. Ceiling Suspension System
61. False ceiling of plasterboard
62. "Aquapanel" type panel
63. "Omega of Knauf" type profile
64. Regularisation of designed waterproof plaster
65. Reinforced concrete wall
66. Thermal insulation with Wallmate 6cm
67. Wardrobe closet
68. Waterproof MDF veneer panel
69. Aluminium bracket
70. Afzelia and new RIGA floor
71. Screed
72. Form layer of lightweight concrete
73. Thermal insulation
74. Plastic screen
75. "Sun-screen" type blind
76. "Vitrocsa" aluminium frame-double rail
77. Afzelia floor
78. Slat
79. Parapet of reinforced concrete
80. Form layer of lightweight concrete

Longitudinal section

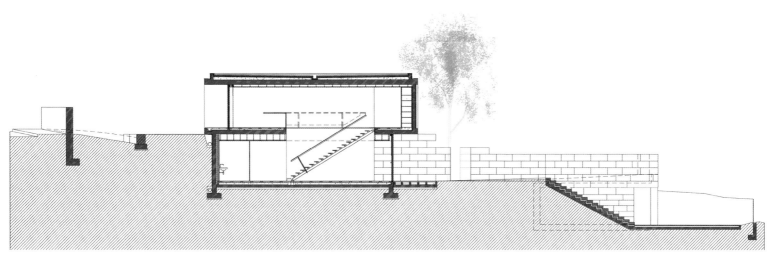

Section 2

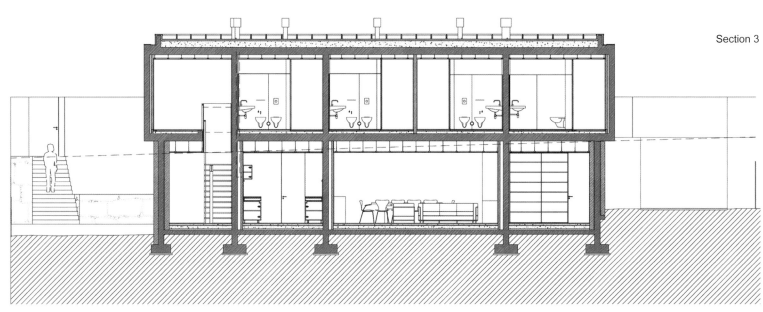

Section 3

230

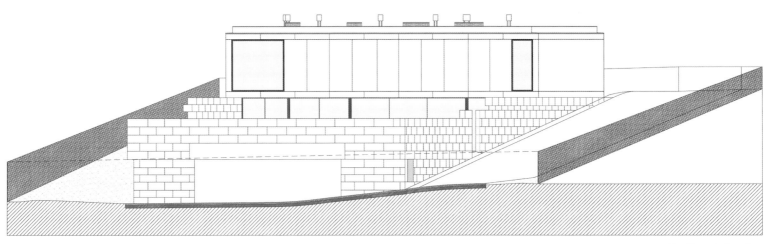

Southwest elevation

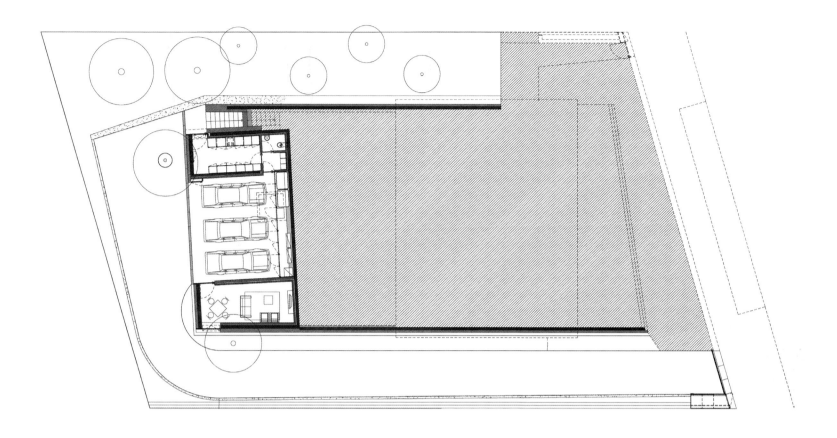

Garage plan

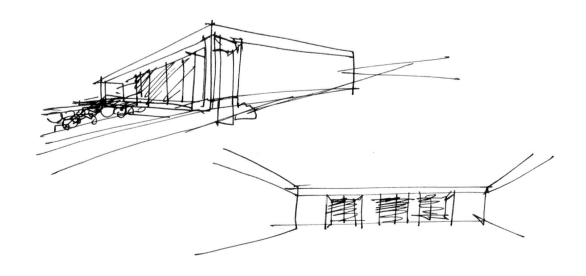

18 Hotelary School in Portalegre

Project Year: 2004
Construction Year: 2007
Location: Portalegre, Portugal
Co-author: Graça Correia
Client: Fundação Robinson
Collaborators: Ana Neto Vieira, Nuno Miguel Ferreira,
Telmo Gervásio Gomes, Ricardo Cardoso, Pedro Gama, Hugo Natário,
Inês Ruas, Rita Breda, Luís Diniz, Nuno Vasconcelos, Ana P. Carvalho,
Ana L. Monteiro, João Marques, Maurícia Bento, Elisama Reis
Structural Consultants: GOP - Gabinete de Organização de Projectos, Lda
Hydraulic Consultants: GOP - Gabinete de Organização de Projectos, Lda
Electrical Consultants: GPIC - Gabinete de Projectos, Consultadoria e Instalações, Lda
Mechanical Consultants: GET - Gestão de Energia Térmica, Lda
Photographer: Luís Ferreira Alves, Christian Richters
Total Area: 4,005 m^2
Site Area: 60,500 m^2

The building of the Hotel and Catering School defines a new street, a structural and vital element to the rehabilitation of the old area of the Robinson Factory. To south, literally "hangs" over the landscape, enjoying the natural slope. The building is intended to be a box resting on the existing embankment defining a large balcony where all main spaces of the school turn to classrooms, library, lounge, restaurant and bar. To north, this box is closed, given its frank relation with the street and sets up two bodies completely closed. The largest and most detached volume embraces all kitchens and infrastructural support to the restaurant, self-service and teaching kitchen, finished in a blue colour traditionally used in bakeries and all places where special hygiene requirements exist. This volume is also denounced by huge skylights-chimneys. At the area in front of the classrooms and corresponding to yellow ochre body are placed the offices and additional spaces of smaller areas, each opening to a small private courtyard on the console. This equipment is an element of articulation with the rest of the urban fabric, serving a good portion of the population.

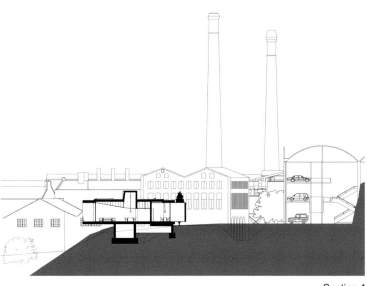

Section 1

236

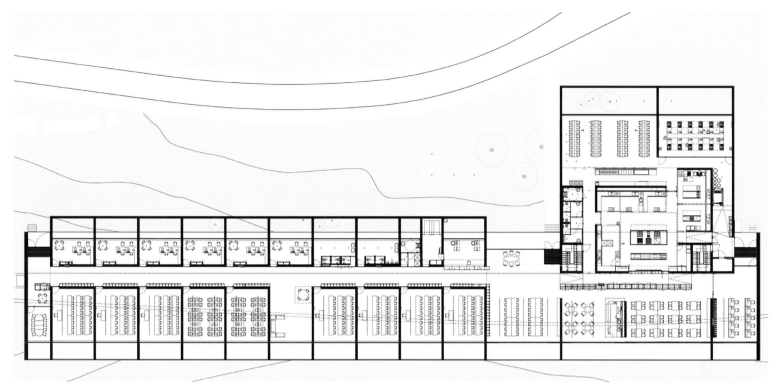

Ground floor plan

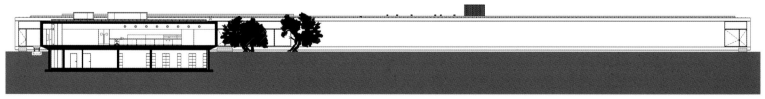

Section 2

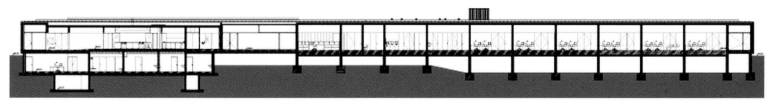

Section 3

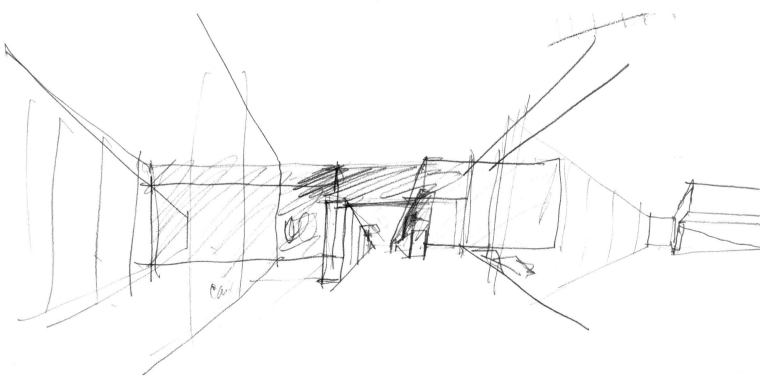

Section 4

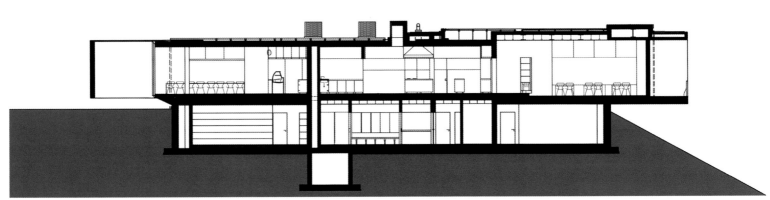

Section 5

⑲ Office Building in Avenida Boavista

Project Year: 2004-2005
Construction Year: 2006-2007
Address: Avenida da Boavista, 4143/4207 e Rua Aristides Sousa Mendes, 181/229
Location: Porto, Portugal
Client: 1946 - Imobiliária, S.A.
Collaborators: José Carlos Mariano, Sílvia Alves, Ricardo Tedim, Luís Peixoto
Structural Consultants: Afassociados
Electrical Consultants: Afassociados
Hydraulic Consultants: Afassociados
Mechanical Consultants: Afassociados
Superviasion: Sopsec, Lda
General Contractor: Edifer
Photographer: Luís Ferreira Alves

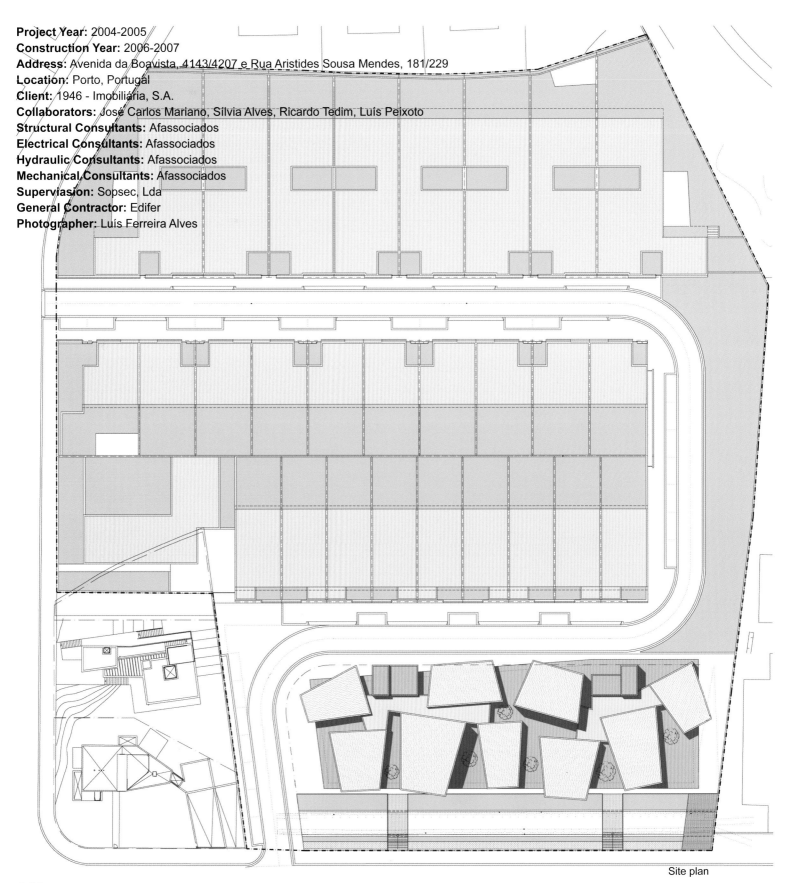

Site plan

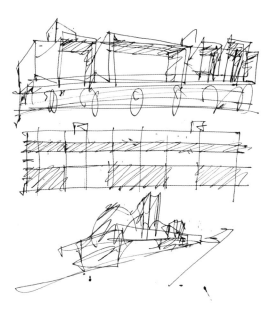

The building is composed by a table parallel to the Avenue, which works as commercial stores. In the tabletop scattered boxes were placed, whose orientation is aimed at the City Park. Those boxes are disposed randomly but interconnected, and function as offices. Different from the traditional platform-like style building that I used to make, now I rethink the concept of the box-like architecture, transforming it into a composition of boxes that generate an urban façade over the avenue. Deployment of its irregularity on the table, resulting interstices, courtyards, gardens - serving each volume, each office, enables us to be "smoking", or feel the proximity of the park, right there in front.

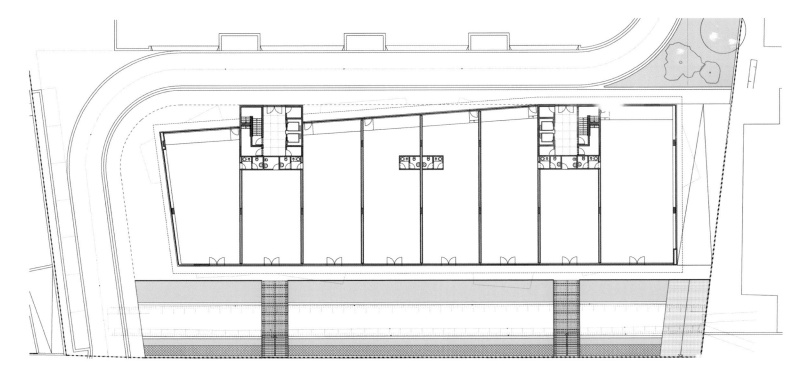

Ground floor plan

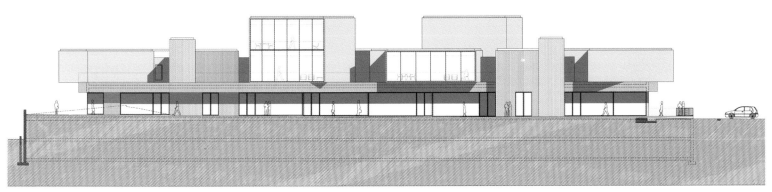

South elevation

Constructive section
1. Zinc plate (Camarinha type)
2. Geotextile
3. Roofmate
4. Regularisation
5. Lightweight concrete
6. Concrete slab
7. False ceiling of plasterboard
8. Linoleum
9. Regularisation
10. Lightweight concrete
11. Concrete slab
12. Stainless steel frames
13. Epoxy mortar
14. Regularisation
15. Lightweight concrete
16. Concrete slab
17. Thermal insulation and zinc ruff
18. Anodised aluminium frames in natural colour
19. Flameproof glass
20. Armed isolation and plaster with paint
21. Concrete paving flags
22. Thermal insulation
23. Concrete
24. Stainless steel guard
25. Granite cube 6x6cm
26. Concrete

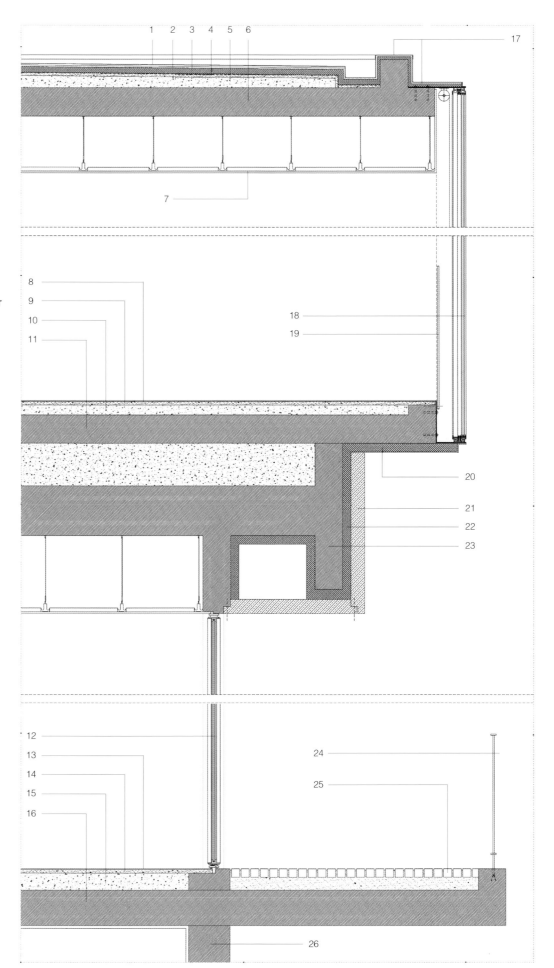

249

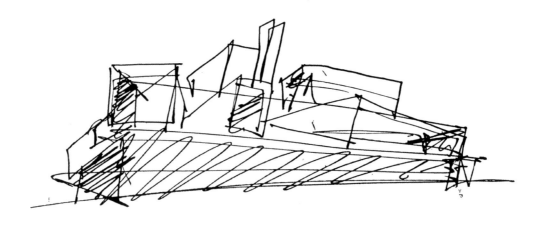

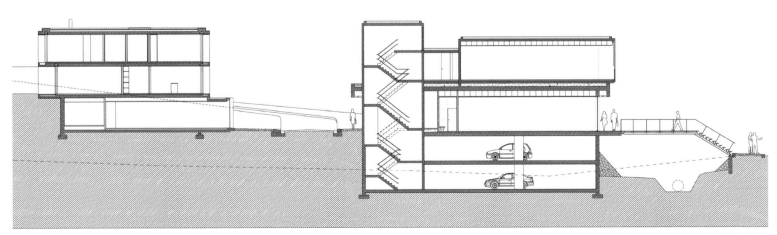

Section 1

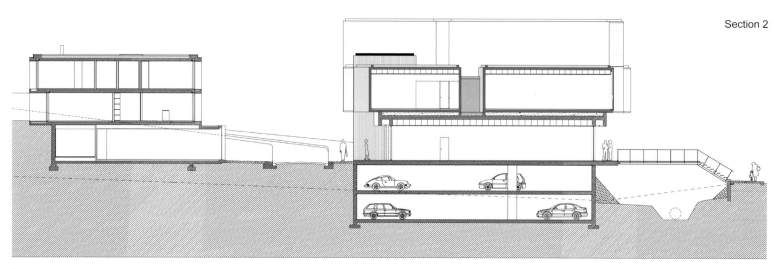

Section 2

252

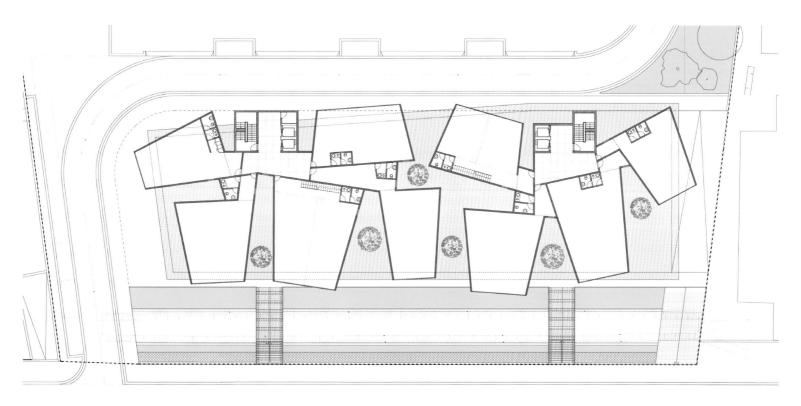

First floor plan

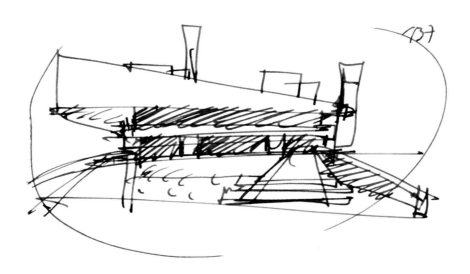

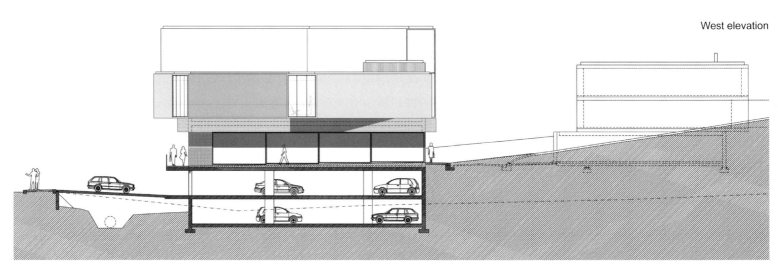

West elevation

20 Paula Rego Museum

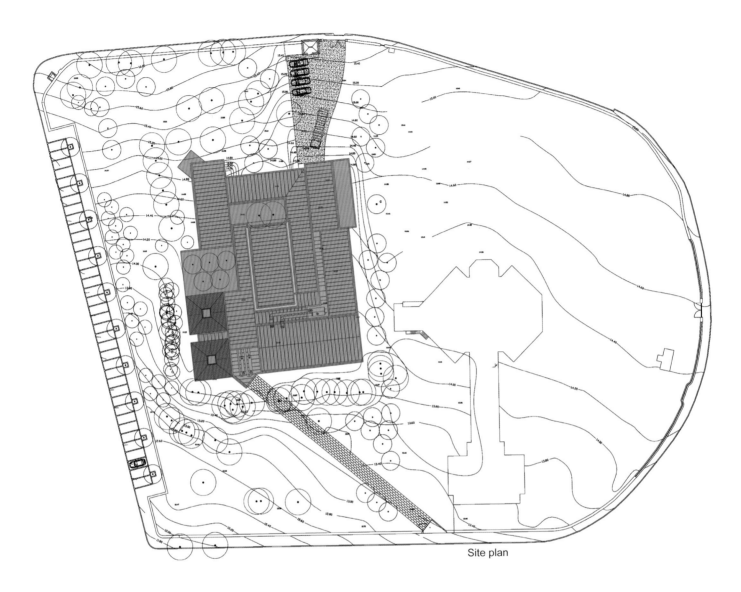

Site plan

Project Year: 2005
Construction Year: 2009
Address: Avenida da República, Cascais
Location: Cascais, Portugal
Client: Cascais City Hall
Project Coordination: Sérgio Koch, Ricardo Prata
Collaborators: Bernardo Monteiro, Diogo Guimarães, Junko Imamura, Kirstin Schätzel, Paula Mesquita, Manuel Vasconcelos, Maria Luís Barros, Pedro G. Oliveira, Rita Alves, Sofia Torres Pereira, Susana Monteiro, Paula Mesquita
Structural Consultants: AFA consult
Hidraulics Consultants: AFA consult
Electrical Consultants: RS – Raul Serafim e associados
Mechanical Consultants: PQF - Paulo Queirós de Faria
Photographer: Luís Ferreira Alves
Site Area: 8,896 m^2
Building Area: 3,307 m^2
Net Area: 2,648 m^2
Cost: 5,000,000 Euros

256

I was so lucky to choose this site, which increased my responsibility after the painter Paula Rêgo had chosen me as projectist. The site was a wood, all surrounded by a wall, with a big empty in the middle, some former club tennis courts, which had disappeared with the Carnation Revolution. With the trees survey, especially their tops, I have developed a set of volumes with different heights, to respond to the plurality of the programme. The boxes distribution works like a mineral positive, from the negative that remains from the tree top perimeter. This "Yang" and "Yin" game between artifact and nature, helped me to decide the exterior material, red concrete, the opposite colour to the green wood, which meanwhile decreased by botanic prophylaxis. As I didn't want the building to be a neutral sum of boxes, I have established a hierarchy, introducing two big pyramids (skylights) in the entrance axis, which are the library and the café, where it wasn't an indifferent Alcobaca's kitchen, some houses from Architect Raul Lino and some illustrations from Boullé. It was my concerning that every exhibition room had always an opening to the exterior, to the garden. It's never too much to oppose the abstract and totally artificial reality of contemporary art to the daily and ruff reality that surrounds us.

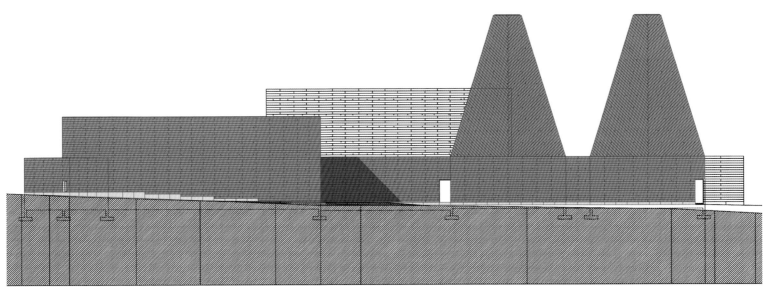

West elevation

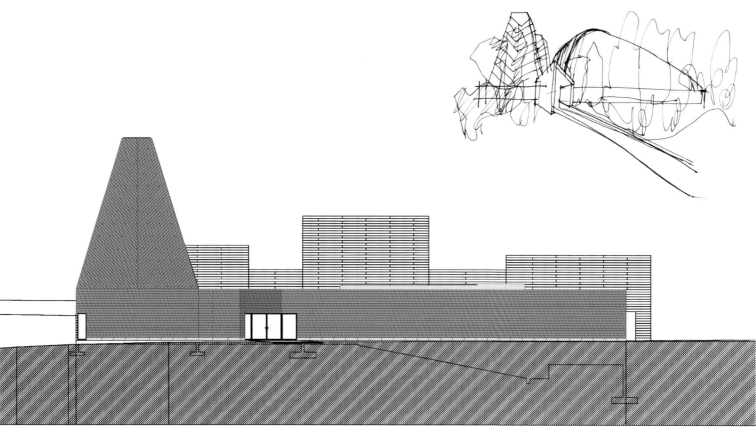

South elevation

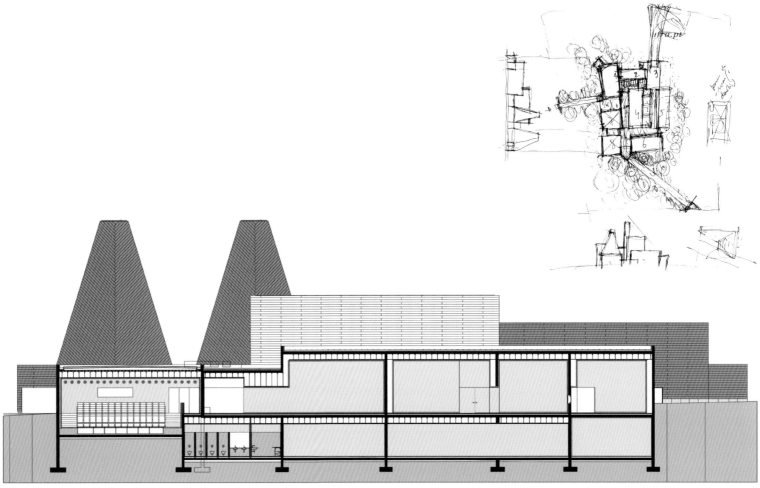

Section 1

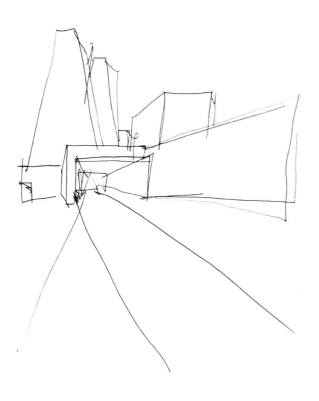

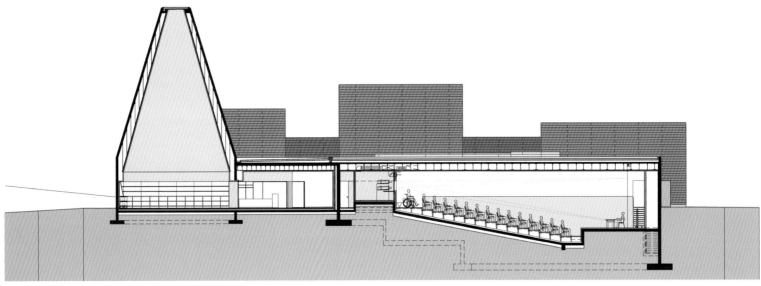

Section 2

Ground floor plan (Right)
1. Courtyard
2. Reception / Coat check
3. Atrium
4. Cafeteria
5. Bar
6. Bookstore
7. Permanent exhibition (Corridor 1)
8. Permanent exhibition (Room 1)
9. Permanent exhibition (Room 2)
10. Permanent exhibition (Room 3)
11. Permanent exhibition (Room 4)
12. Permanent exhibition (Room 5)
13. Permanent exhibition (Room 6)
14. Temporary exhibition
15. Corridor 2
16. Projection booth
17. Translation booth
18. Storage
19. Auditorium
20. Stairs
21. Offices
22. Loading and unloading
23. Technical courtyard

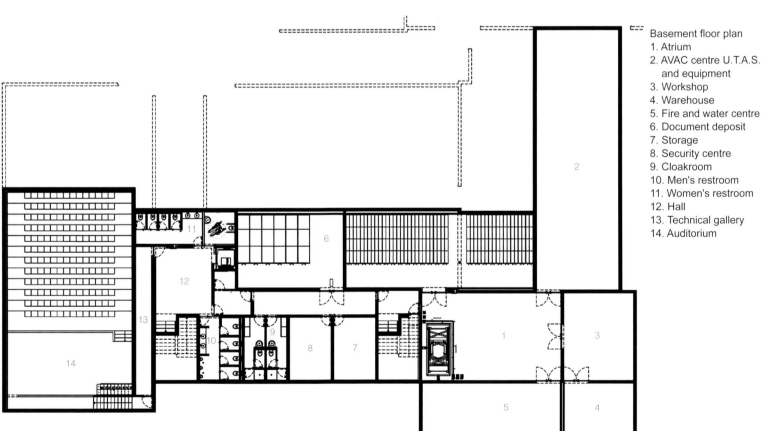

Basement floor plan
1. Atrium
2. AVAC centre U.T.A.S. and equipment
3. Workshop
4. Warehouse
5. Fire and water centre
6. Document deposit
7. Storage
8. Security centre
9. Cloakroom
10. Men's restroom
11. Women's restroom
12. Hall
13. Technical gallery
14. Auditorium

Constructive section

1. Zinc plate roof cover
2. Plasterboard 20mm
3. Acoustic ceiling
4. Joint 5mm
5. Azulino de Cascais marble 30mm
6. Cement mortar
7. Levelling layer
8. Reinforced cement mortar
9. Lightweight aggregate filling
10. Zinc water drain
11. Plasterboard 20mm
12. Acoustic ceiling
13. Joint 5 mm
14. Lacquered MDF wardrobe
15. Rockwool 60mm
16. Double height density plasterboard
17. White marble skirting board (60mm)

18. Zinc cover
19. Skylight
20. Azulino de Cascais Marble 30mm
21. Cement mortar
22. Levelling layer
23. Reinforced cement mortar
24. Lightweight aggregate filling
25. Zinc water drain
26. Drain
27. Plasterboard 20mm
28. Acoustic ceiling
29. Joint 5mm
30. "Aleixo" lamps
31. Rockwool 60mm
32. Double height density plasterboard
33. White marble skirting board
34. Joint 5mm

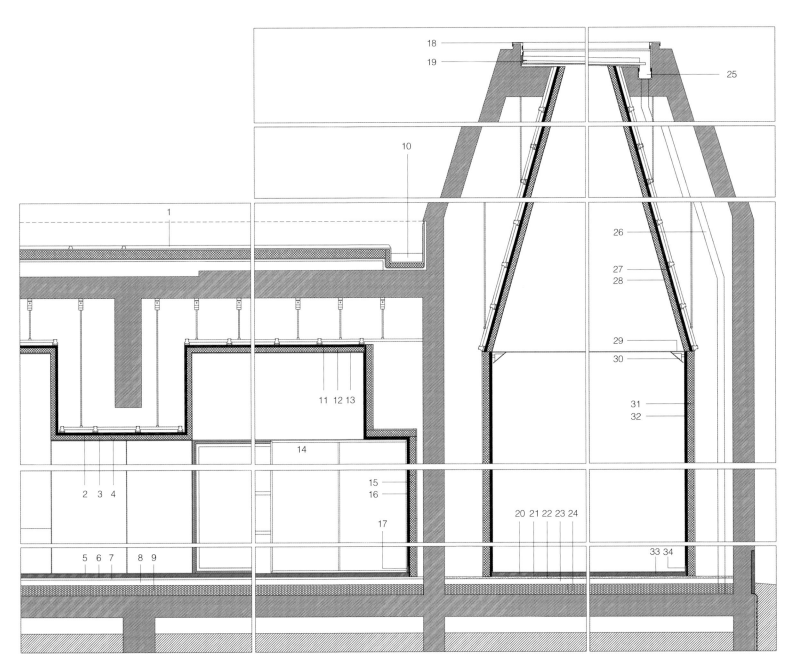

FACT SUMMARY

Eduardo Souto de Moura
Born on 25th July, 1952 in Oporto, Portugal

EDUCATION

School of Architecture (ESBAP), Oporto, Portugal

BRIEF CHRONOLOGY

1974	Worked with architect Noé Dinis
1975-1979	Worked with architect Alvaro Siza
1980-1991	Assistant Professor, Faculty of Architecture, Oporto University, Portugal
1980	Opened his own architectural firm

CHRONOLOGY OF MAJOR WORKS

1980-1984	Municipal Market, Braga, Portugal
1981-1991	"Casa das Artes", S.E.C. Cultural Centre Porto, Portugal
1982-1985	House One, Nevogilde, Oporto, Portugal
1983-1988	House Two, Nevogilde, Oporto, Portugal
1984-1989	House in Quinta do Lago, Almansil, Algarve, Portugal
1985	Bridge "Dell' Academia" La Biennale di Venezia, Venice, Italy
1986-1988	Annexes to a house in Rua da Vilarinha, Oporto, Portugal
1987-1992	House in Alcanena, Torres Novas, Portugal
1987-1989	Salzburg Hotel Competition
1987	Master Plan for "Porta dei Colli" Palermo, Italy (Milan Triennal)
1987-1991	House 1 in Miramar, Vila Nova de Gaia, Portugal
1987-1994	House in Av. da Boavista, Porto, Portugal
1988	Master Plan and Civic Buildings for "Mondello", Palermo, Italy
1989-1997	Conversion of the Santa Maria do Bouro Convent into a State Inn, Amares, Portugal
1989-1994	House in "Bom Jesus", Braga, Portugal
1990-1994	Geo-Sciences Department, University of Aveiro, Aveiro, Portugal
1990-1993	House in Maia, Maia, Portugal House in Baião, Baião, Portugal
1991-1995	House in Tavira, Tavira, Algarve, Portugal
1997-2007	Burgo Project in Boavista Avenue (Office Blocks and Commercial Mall), Porto, Portugal
1991-1998	House in Moledo, Caminha, Portugal
1992-1995	Apartment Block in Rua do "Teatro", Porto, Portugal
1992-2000	Children's Library and Auditorium, Porto, Portugal
1993-2004	Remodelling and Improvement of the Grão Vasco Museum, Viseu, Portugal
1993-1999	Courtyard Houses in Matosinhos, Matosinhos, Portugal
1993-2007	Conversion of the Customs Building into Transports and Communications Museum, Porto, Portugal
1994-2002	House in Serra da Arrábida, Portugal House in Cascais, Portugal
1994-2001	Residential Building, Liege Square, Porto, Portugal
1995-2004	Master Plan for Maia City, Maia, Portugal
1995-2002	Conversion Plan for the Coastline of South Matosinhos Matosinhos, Portugal
1995-1998	Design of the Portuguese Pavilion, Expo 1998, Lisbon, Portugal
1996-1997	Interior Project for Santa Maria do Bouro Inn, Amares, Portugal
1997-1999	Interior Project for the "Armazens do Chiado", Lisbon, Portugal
1997-2001	Portuguese Photographic Centre, "Edificio da Cadeia da Relação do Porto", Porto, Portugal
1997-2005	Architectural Project for the Porto Metro (subway) Porto, Portugal
1997-2001	Residential building in Cidade da Maia, Maia, Portugal
1997-2001	Remodelling of the Market in Braga, Braga, Portugal
1998-1999	Cultural "Silo" in the Norteshopping, Matosinhos, Portugal
1998-2003	Cinema House for Manoel de Oliveira, Oporto, Portugal
1999-2000	Co-author with Alvaro Siza of the Portuguese Pavilion for Expo Hannover
2000	Multi-purpose pavilion in Viana do Castelo, Portugal
2000-2003	Architecture Project for the Braga Stadium, Braga, Portugal
2002-2006	28 Houses in na Av.da Boavista, Porto, Portugal
2002	Rehabilitation of the Historical Centre Valença do Minho, Portugal
2003-2008	Modern Contemporary Art Museum in Bragança, Portugal

2003	House in Girona, Llabia, Barcelona, Spain
	Co-author with Alvaro Siza of the Metro Station
	Municipio - Linea 1, Naples, Italy
2004-2005	Co-author with Alvaro Siza of the Serpentine
	Pavilion, London, UK
2004	Golf Resort, Óbidos, Portugal
2004	Co-author with Atelier Terradas i Muntañola for
	Residential Centre and Services - La Pallaresa,
	Barcelona, Spain
2005-2009	Paula Rêgo Museum, Cascais, Portugal
2005	Office Building for Novartis, Basil, Switzerland
2005	Bernia Golf Resort, Alicante, Spain
	Kortrijk Crematorium, Belgium
2006	House of Professor, Cascais, Portugal
	Two Family Houses, Ibiza, Spain
2007	Conversion of "Convento das Bernardas" into
	Family Houses, Tavira, Portugal
	Office Building for Edemi Gardens, Porto,
	Portugal
	Residential Building for Vale de Santo Amaro
	Alcântara, Lisbon, Portugal
	Wine Cellar in Mealhada, Portugal
	Master Plan for New City Hall Buidling, Trofa,
	Portugal
	Tower in Benidorm, Apartments and Hotel,
	Spain
	Espaço Miguel Torga, Sabrosa, Portugal
	Conversion of Pensão Monumental into
	Apartments, Porto, Portugal
2008	Co-author with Ângelo de Sousa for
	the Portuguese Official Representation in the
	Venice Biennale 2008, Venice, Italy
	Hotel in Obidos, Obidos, Portugal
	Co-author with Architect Flávio Barbini for the
	Recuperation of Pagnoni Complex, Monza, Italy

SELECTED PUBLISHED MATERIALS

In Books   "Souto de Moura", Gustavo Gili, Barcelona, 1990
"Eduardo Souto Moura", Blau Editora, Lisbon, 1994
"Ten Houses", Rockport Publishers,
Massachusetts, 1998
"Santa Maria do Bouro", White & Blue, Lisbon, 2001
"Eduardo Souto Moura", Blau Editora, Lisbon, 2000
"Eduardo Souto Moura", Electa, Milan, 2003
"Eduardo Souto Moura", Gustavo Gili,
Barcelona, 2003
"Eduardo Souto Moura", LOFT Publications,
Barcelona, 2003
"Stein Element Stone", Werner Blaser,
Birhauser Publishers, Basel, 2003
"Casa do Cinema Manoel de Oliveira",
Caleidoscópio, Casal de Cambra, 2004
"Pavilhão Multiusos Viana do Castelo",
Civilização, Porto, 2005
"Estádio Municipal de Braga", Civilização,
Porto, 2007

"Conversas com Estudantes", Gustavo Gili,
Barcelona, 2008
"Conversaciones con Estudantes", Gustavo Gili,
Barcelona, 2008
"Eduardo Souto de Moura 2008", Caleidoscópio,
Casal de Cambra, 2008
"Eduardo Souto de Moura-Architect",
Loft Publications, Barcelona, 2009
"Casa das Histórias Paula Rego", City Hall Cascais,
2009
"Eduardo Souto Moura - Architect", Bertrand / (LOFT),
Lisbon, 2010

In Reviews   "Architecti" nº 5, Trifório Editora, Lisbon, 1990
Review "2G nº 5", Gustavo Gili. Barcelona, 1998
"du" nº 715, Herzog, Zurique, 2001
"A&B" nº3, Watekz Kamienia, 2002
"Arquitectura" nº 337, COAM, Madrid, 3ºTrimestre 2004
"Estádio Municipal de Braga", City Hall Braga, Braga,
2004
"Obra Reciente", TC-Cuadernos Tribuna de la
Construcción nº 64, Valencia 2004
"El Croquis" nº 124, El Croquis, Madrid 2005
"AA - Arquitecturas de Auto" r nº32, T 6 Ediciones,
Pamplona 2005
"A+202-Revue Belge d'Architecture", Bruxelles 2006
Bauwelt nº 37, Bau, Berlin 2008
Cdo-Cadernos d' Obra nº01, Gequaltec / Feup, Porto
2009
WA nº229, School of Architecture Tsinghua, China, 2009
"SOUTO DE MOURA 2005-2009", El Croquis nº 146,
Madrid 2009
"ArchiNews" nº 16, Eduardo Souto de Moura, inside city,
Lisbon, 2010

In Catalogues   Temi di Progetti, Accademia di Architettura,
Mendrisio 1998
Case / Ultimi Progetti, Bolonha Città Europea de la
Cultura, 2000
"Prémio Secil de Arquitectura 2004", O A, Secil,
Lisbon 2005
"BURGO – O Projecto", Grupo San Jose, Porto 2005
"BOM SUCESSO - Design Resort, Leisure, Golf & Spa",
Acordo, Porto 2006
"Vinte e Duas Casas", (VI Bienal de São Paulo 2005),
OA & Caleidoscópio, Lisbon, 2006
"Princípio e Fim de Um Projecto - Souto Moura /
Ferreira Alves" JN/DN, Porto 2008
Architecture and Photography Exhibition
"Uma Conversa no campo com ESM", Colecções
Privadas, Museu Municipal de Tavira
"Cá fora: arquitectura desassossegada", Eduardo
Souto de Moura / Ângelo de Sousa
Veneza 2008 - La Biennale di Venezia-11ª Mostra
"CASA DAS HISTÓRIAS, CA: 05", City Hall Cascais,
Cascais 2009

269

AWARDS

1980   António de Almeida Foundation
1981   1ˢᵗ prize in the competition for the Cultural Centre of the S.E.C., Oporto, Portugal
1982   1ˢᵗ prize in the competition for the Restructuring of the Main Square in Évora, Portugal
1984   Antero de Quental Foundation
1986   1ˢᵗ prize in the competition for the C.I.A.C. pavilions
1987   1ˢᵗ prize in the competition for a Hotel in Salzburg
1990   1ˢᵗ prize (ex-aequo) in the IN / ARCH 1990 per la Sicilia
1992   Secil Award for Architecture
         1ˢᵗ prize in the competition for the "Construction of an Auditorium and a Children's Library in the City Hall Library", Oporto, Portugal
1993   2ⁿᵈ prize in the competition for "The Stone in Architecture"
         Secil Award for Architecture - Honourable Mention for the House in Alcanena
         National Awards for Architecture - Honourable Mention for the Cultural Centre and the House in Alcanena
1995   International Prize for Stone in Architecture Fiera di Verona, for the House in "Bom Jesus", Braga
1996   Annual Award of the Portuguese Department of the International Association of Art Critics, for the building in Rua do Teatro
         Nominee for the "Mies van der Rohe European Union Architecture Prize" for the following projects:
         1990 - Cultural Centre, Oporto
         1992 - House in Alcanena
         1994 - Department of Geosciences, Aveiro University
         1996 - Building in Rua do Teatro, Oporto
         1998 - Pousada of Santa Maria do Bouro
         2000 - Courtyard Houses in Matosinhos
         2002 - Cinema House "Manoel de Oliveira", Oporto
         2010 - Paula Rego's House of Stories, Cascais
1998   Nominee for the Award IBERFAD with the "Pousada Santa Maria do Bouro"
         1ˢᵗ prize in the I Bienal Iberoamericana with the "Pousada Santa Maria do Bouro"
         Award Pessoa
1999   Award "Stone in Architecture" - Honourable Mention for the "Pousada Santa Maria do Bouro"
         Award FAD - Opinion Award for the "Silo Cultural" in Norteshopping, Matosinhos
2001   Award Heinrich-Tessenow-Medal in Gold
2002   Nominee for the "III Bienal Iberoamericana de Arquitectura e Ingenieria Civil", for the Courtyard Houses in Matosinhos
2003   Award "Stone in Architecture" - Honourable Mention of the Project in Matosinhos South
2004   Finalist of the FAD Award 2004, for the project "2 Houses in Ponte de Lima" - Opinion Award of the FAD Jury 2004
         Secil Award for Architecture
2005   Finalist of the Prize "Prémio Europeu de Arquitectura Pabellón Mies van der Rohe 2004" for the project of the "Braga Stadium".

Award FAD, Barcelona, for the project of Braga Stadium
Opinion Award FAD, Barcelona, for the project of Braga Stadium
Gold Medal for Braga Stadium - IAKS, International Association for Sports and Leisure Facilities, Cologne, Germany
Finalist of the "I Prémio de Arquitectura Ascensores Enor", for the project "Cinema House Manoel de Oliveira"
1ˢᵗ Prize in the competition for a Crematorium in Kortrijk, Belgium
2006   Architecture International Prize for "Braga Municipal Stadium" from the Chicago Athenaeum Museum, USA
         Honourable Mention for "Braga Municipal Stadium"
         "Best Window" VETECO, Madrid Fair, Spain
         FAD Award "Ciutat i Paisatge" with the Project "Metro do Porto"
         ENOR Ward of Portugal with the Project "Metro do Porto"
         "Gran Prémio Enor" with the Project "Metro do Porto"
         "Finalist" for the Jury of Enor Award with the Project "Metro do Porto"
         Honourable Mention for "Braga Municipal Stadium"
         V Edition Bienal Iberoamericana of Architecture and Urbanism, Montevideo, Uruguay
2007   Honourary Fellow of the American Institute of Architects (AIA)
2008   Architecture International Prize for "Burgo Office Tower" from the Chicago Athenaeum Museum, USA
         International Fellow of Royal Institute of British Architects - RIBA
         Finalist of FAD Award 2008 for "Burgo Tower"
2009   Green Good Design 2009, with the "Luce 3" Lamp
         The European Centre for Architecture Art Design and Urban Studies and the Chicago Athenaeum
         Award "Cidades de Excelência 2008-2009", for the project "Plano de Pormenor do Largo do Souto, em S. João da Madeira"
         Doctor Honoris Causa, Universidade de Chiclayo, República do Perú
         Architecture International Prize for "Contemporary Art Museum of Bragança" from the Chicago Athenaeum Museum, USA
         First prize in the Competition for the project "Railway High Speed Axis Lisbon / Madrid - PPP1 - Poceirão / Caia", co-authored with Arch. Adriano Pimenta
         First prize in the competition for the New Hospital of Évora
         First Prize in the "Project LIWA" an Oasis of Learning for Abu Dhabi, United Arab Emirates
2010   Nominated as a Member of the Academy of Arts Architecture Section of Berlin
         Architecture Medal of "L'Academie d'Architecture de France", Paris
         Award for the project "Paula Rego Museum" from The Chicago Athenaeum, the Museum of Architecture and Design and the European Centre for Architecture Art Design and Urban Studies

EXHIBITIONS

1983	"After the Modernism", National Society of Beaux Arts, in Lisbon
	"11 Oporto Architects - Recent Images", S.N.B.A., Lisbon; House of Crivos, Braga;
	Coop. Árvore, Porto
	"Architecture Drawings", Architectural Association, London.
	"Braga Market", Biennale of Paris.
1985	"House 2 in Nevogilde", Identita nell'Arquittectura, Pirano, Jugoslávia
1987	"Corbu vu par...", I.F.A., Paris
	Milan Triennale
	"The Scholl of Oporto", Clermond-Ferrand, France
1988	"Furniture Exhibition", Atalaia Store, Lisbon
	"Italian Design Forum", Milan and New York
	"Emerging European Architects", Univ. Harvard, Boston; Univ. Columbia, Nova York.
1989	"Lieux d'Architecture Europeénne", Academy of France in Rome
1990	"Architectures Publiques", Centre Georges Pompidou, Paris
	"Ouvertures a Bordeaux", Arc en Rêve - Centre d'Architecture, Bordeaux
1992	"Installation", Architektur Forum Zurich, Zurich.
	"10 Portuguese Authors - Contemporary Design", House of Arts, Oporto
1993	"Portugal Four Points of View", Galerija DESSA, Ljubljana
1994	"Waves of Influence", New York, USA
	"Projects and Materials", Cultural Centre of Belém, Lisbon
1996	"Object Light", Porto and Lisbon
	"Less is More", UIA, Colegio Arquitectos Catalunya, Barcelona
1997	"From Project till Construction", City Hall of Maia, Maia
	"Design aus Portugal - eine Anthologie, in Frankfurt
1998	"Temi di progetti", Art Museum in Mendrísio, Switzerland
	"Temi di progetti", E.P.F.L., Lausanne, Switzerland
	"Temi di progetti", gta institut, Zurich, Switzerland
1999	"Temi di progetti", Vicenza, Italy
	"Temi di Progetti", City Hall in Matosinhos, Matosinhos
2001	"Case. Ultimi Progetti", Bologna, Italy
	"Case. Ultimi Progeti", Dresden, Germany
2002	Exhibition in Stuttgart
	Exhibition of Contemporary Design, Helsinki, Finland
2003	Exhibition in Pamplona, Spain
2004	"Draws in the Cities: Portuguese Architecture", V BIA of S. Paulo, Brasil
	"Draws in the Cities: Portuguese Architecture", Milan Triennale
	"EURO 2004 Stadiums", Lusíada University, in Lisbon
	Milan Triennale
	"Secil Award of Architecture 2004", Portuguese Architects Association, Lisbon
	Participation in Venice Biennale
2005	"Inedited 2005", drawings exhibition, House of Madrid, Spain
	Participation in the exhibition about no constructed projects, Fribourg, Switzerland
	Participation in S. Paulo Biennale, Brasil
2006	"22 Houses" in Portuguese Architects Association, Lisbon
	Participation in the exhibition "Inhabit Portugal 2003 / 2005",
	Cultural Centre of Belém, Lisbon
2007	Exhibition "Work Meeting North #005 dedicated to the theme
	Urban Infra-structures - Oporto Metro 1994
	to 2005, Transports Museum in Oporto
	Architecture Triennale of Lisbon
2008	Eduardo Souto de Moura / Luis Ferreira Alves -
	Exhibition in the Gallery of the Journal "Notícias", in Porto
2009	Architecture: Portugal out of Portugal, Berlin

©2010 by Design Media Publishing Limited
This edition published in November 2011

Design Media Publishing Limited
20/F Manulife Tower
169 Electric Rd, North Point
Hong Kong
Tel: 00852-28672587
Fax: 00852-25050411
E-mail: Kevinchoy@designmediahk.com
www.designmediahk.com

Planning: Lukas Sun
Editing: Joana de Mira Corrêa
Proofreading: Qian Yin
Design/Layout: Chunling Yang

ISBN 978-988-15071-9-8

Printed in China